D1486475

Freedom of Information

A practical guide to
implementing the Act

Freedom of Information

A practical guide to
implementing the Act

Kelvin Smith

facet publishing

© Kelvin Smith 2004

Published by
Facet Publishing
7 Ridgmount Street
London WC1E 7AE

Facet Publishing (formerly Library Association Publishing) is wholly owned by CILIP: the Chartered Institute of Library and Information Professionals.

First published 2004

British Library Cataloguing in Publication Data
A catalogue record for this book is available from the British Library.

ISBN 1-85604-517-X

Typeset in 10/13pt Revival 565 and Zurich by Facet Publishing.
Printed and made in Great Britain by MPG Books Ltd, Bodmin, Cornwall.

Contents

Acknowledgements

I have been immersed (it seems) in the subject of freedom of information for the last six years. During that time there have been many people who have given me information, opportunity and inspiration to pursue the matter vigorously. I would like to make special mention of the following.

I am particularly indebted to Susan Healy, Head of the Information Legislation Unit at the National Archives. I have called upon her vast knowledge of information legislation, particularly FOI, on numerous occasions. She is far more expert on the legislation than I, and I hope that she will forgive any lack of clarity that may have crept into this work.

Christine Gifford and Dilys Jones, both members of the Lord Chancellor's Advisory Group on implementation of the Freedom of Information Act, and more recently the embodiment of Public Partners, a new organization set up to provide education and training to the public sector in the area of FOI and other information management issues, have given me plenty of opportunity to put forward my views and to train and advise others in many aspects of FOI. I am very grateful for their encouragement and support.

While this book has been completed entirely in my own time, I have to acknowledge the help that I have been able to call on from the National Archives. They have provided the framework and context for much of the content.

Introduction

This work takes its title very seriously. It is a practical guide to the implementation of the Freedom of Information Act 2000 (FOI Act). Its combination of descriptions, checklists, models and practical examples will enable all those involved in the discharge of this important enactment to do so without fear or worry. It tries to get away from describing freedom of information in legal terms and tries to focus on the implementation of the Freedom of Information Act from a user's point of view. It is not meant to provide an analysis of the legislation, in which there are very many micro-provisions, but rather to point the reader to those parts of the Act which will affect implementation procedures. It leaves the reader to follow up the detailed points and issues. This does not mean that practitioners can get away without reading the Act and, indeed, where there is any doubt about the legal position, the Act must be consulted.

Who will benefit from this guide? Potentially, freedom of information legislation will affect every person employed in public services work. Certainly those involved in customer enquiries, record keeping and policy making will be directly affected. Public services include:

- central government departments and agencies
- non-departmental public bodies (NDPBs)
- local authorities – all tiers, down to parish councils
- higher education and further education organizations
- schools
- police authorities
- National Health Service.

In addition, the FOI Act itself mentions over 450 bodies which are regarded as public authorities for the purposes of the Act. These range from various official advisory and expert committees to regulators and organizations such as the Parole Board, the General Medical Council and the Higher Education Funding Councils. In essence, if an organization discharges a public function (and this may well include some parts of the private sector), it will be covered by the legislation. This guide uses the term 'public authority' or 'authority' throughout to describe all those organizations covered by the Freedom of Information Act.

The relationship between government and citizen in the United Kingdom will experience a fundamental change on 1 January 2005. On that date the Freedom of Information Act 2000 (in Scotland the Freedom of Information (Scotland) 2002 Act) becomes fully effective.[1] These may seem to be simply more pieces of legislation from the parliamentary process but it is legislation that is at the heart of the delivery of public services in the United Kingdom.

The Freedom of Information (Scotland) Act 2002 is broadly similar to the UK legislation. The Scottish Executive and the Scottish Information Commissioner have agreed a timetable which means that, like the UK Act, the legislation will be fully implemented on 1 January 2005. The Scottish Act applies to Scottish public authorities, which include:

- the Scottish Executive and its agencies
- local authorities
- NHS Scotland
- schools, colleges and universities
- police
- the Scottish Parliament.

As part of the devolution settlement, UK Government departments operating in Scotland and cross-border public authorities (such as the Ministry of Defence and the Forestry Commission) are not covered by Scottish FOI legislation but instead by the UK Act.

A good overview of the Freedom of Information (Scotland) Act 2002 can be found on the website of the Scottish Executive: www.scotland.gov.uk/government/foi.

The legislation is the culmination of almost 50 years of debate on the rights of individuals to be able to access information about the way in which they are governed and the way in which decisions affecting their lives are made. The debate has been influenced by many factors – legislation in other countries, the Campaign for Freedom of Information, the Government's commitment to improved public services, and the pressure for greater openness and transparency in government. This influence also works the other way – much of the work in developing the legislation has affected those processes that are needed to make it work. All this is examined in Chapter 1, 'Background to the Freedom of Information Act'.

The Act embraces the whole of the public sector and some parts of the private sector which discharge public functions. It imposes significant duties and responsibilities on these organizations. They need to:

- know what information they hold
- manage their information holdings effectively
- have in place the infrastructure for dealing with FOI requests
- meet challenging deadlines in responding to individual requests for information
- proactively disseminate information through a publication scheme

- set up arrangements to handle complaints and appeals
- ensure consistency in discharging their duties under the Act.

They must also undertake many other tasks resulting from these main duties. Descriptions and analyses of these responsibilities are covered by Chapter 2, 'The legislation'. Subsequent chapters examine the principal elements of the Act, namely exemptions, publication schemes and enforcement.

The Freedom of Information legislation will only be as good as the quality of the records which are subject to its provisions. Statutory rights of access such as this are of little use if reliable records and information are not created in the first place, if they cannot be found when needed, or if the arrangements for their eventual archiving or destruction are inadequate. In addition the fast-growing use of information technology will increase the pressure on the record-keeping system. Good records management practice is therefore essential in implementing the Act. Chapter 6, 'Records management', examines this area.

Freedom of Information is affected by several other enactments, most notably the Data Protection Act 1998 and the Human Rights Act 1998 as well as by secondary legislation such as the Environmental Information Regulations. The relationships between these can be difficult and can seem contradictory. An attempt is made in Chapter 7, 'Data protection, human rights and other legislation', to make these clearer.

In keeping with the practical nature of this work Chapter 8, 'Staffing and training', provides a description of what needs to be done to enable staff and public alike to understand and be able to use the Act fully. It includes a competency framework and model training schemes.

The final chapter, 'Getting ready for Freedom of Information', gives some practical advice on what needs to be done in the immediate future to ensure that public authorities are well prepared to implement the legislation in January 2005 and beyond.

Three appendices provide copies of the Codes of Practice authorized by the Freedom of Information Act, definitions of terms used in the Act and in related material, and further sources of advice and guidance.

Finally, an important caveat. The advice and guidance in this book does not constitute legal advice. In any cases of doubt over the legislative or legal position, readers are advised to consult with their legal representatives.

Note

1   Henceforth the phrase 'FOI Act', 'the Act' or similar expressions refer to both Freedom of Information Acts.

1

Background to the Freedom of Information Act

This chapter provides a brief description of legislation and attempts at legislation from the beginning of the twentieth century to make government information more available. It also describes Codes of Practice on openness currently in force and more recent moves to bring the legislation forward.

Bills, Acts and Regulations

In modern times the culture of secrecy in government began with the Official Secrets Act 1911. This was designed to prevent the disclosure of official documents and information. Over 60 years later, in the Queen's Speech debate of 1976, the Government announced that it was its intention in the future to publish as much as possible of the factual and analytical material used as background to major policy studies. In the following year, on 6 July 1977, Sir Douglas Allen, Head of the Home Civil Service, wrote a letter to the heads of all government departments advising them of changes for making more official information available to the public. The letter, which became known as the Croham Directive (after Sir Douglas became Lord Croham), said:

> The change may seem simply to be one of degree and timing. But it is intended to mark a real change of policy, even if the initial step is modest. In the past it has normally been assumed that background material relating to policy studies and reports would not be published unless the responsible Minister or Ministers decided otherwise.
>
> Henceforth, the working assumption should be that material will be published unless they decide that it should not be.

Although it was the general view that the Directive worked for a few months, while it was still in the minds of officials, and very quickly fell into disuse, it seemed to have been the catalyst for greater pressure to release official information, not least from the Campaign for Freedom of Information. Shortly after the Directive there were several Acts of Parliament and other regulations granting limited access rights to different types of information (see Table 1.1).

Table 1.1 Legislation granting limited access rights to information

Title and date	Coverage
Data Protection Act 1984	Rights granted to individuals to see information about themselves held on computers
Local Government (Access to Information) Act 1985	Local council meetings, reports and papers
Access to Personal Files Act 1987	Manually held social work and housing records
Access to Medical Records Act 1988	Reports produced by a doctor for an employer or insurance company
Environment and Safety Information Act 1988	Enforcement notices when organizations breach laws dealing with environmental protection and safety
Land Registration Act 1988	Access to the Land Register
Official Secrets Act 1989	Repeal of section 2 of the Official Secrets Act 1911, replaced by provision to protect information about security, international relations, defence, and law enforcement
Environmental Protection Act 1990	Access to various pollution registers
Access to Health Records Act 1990	Information in medical records
Environmental Information Regulations 1992	Environmental information
Open Government Code of Practice 1994	Access to government information
Code of Practice on Openness in the National Health Service 1995	Information about the services provided by the NHS, including costs, quality standards and performance against targets
Public Interest Disclosure Act 1998	Protection of individuals who make certain disclosures of information in the public interest (and connected purposes)
Local Government Act 2000	Requirement on local authorities to: • issue monthly forward plans showing forthcoming decisions and listing related documents • give a minimum of three days' prior access to reports, agenda and background papers for decisions • ensure that meetings at which 'key decisions' are to be discussed or taken are open to the public • produce a record of such decisions and the reasoning behind them
Local Authorities (Executive Arrangements) (Access to Information) (England) Regulations 2000	Access to local government information

There were also several attempts and promises to introduce Bills on access to information (see Table 1.2).

Table 1.2 Bills on access to information

Date	Introduced By	Outcome
1978	Clement Freud	Fell when the 1979 election was called
1981	Frank Hooley	Opposed by the Government; defeated at second reading
1984	David Steel	Abandoned
1991	Archy Kirkwood	Did not reach second reading
1992	Shadow government	Promised to introduce if elected
1992	Mark Fisher	Talked out after Committee stage
1998	Andrew Mackinlay	Abandoned
1998	Lord Lucas of Crudwell	Abandoned

Codes of Practice

The White Paper *Open Government*, published in July 1993, set out proposals for new legislation and for a Code of Practice on Access to Government Information. The Code was introduced in 1994, and revised in 1997, but the accompanying legislation never saw the light of day. In subsequent years similar Codes of Practice were introduced for the Welsh Assembly, Scottish Executive and the National Health Service. These Codes of Practice – which remain in force until the Freedom of Information Act is fully implemented – all have the same basic premise, stated in their introductions, albeit in slightly different ways:

> *This Code of Practice sets out the basic principles underlying public access to information about the NHS. It reflects the Government's intention to ensure greater access by the public to information about public services and complements the Code of Access to Information which applies to the Department of Health, including the NHS Executive. . . . The aims of the Code are to ensure that people:*

> - *have access to available information about the services provided by the NHS, the cost of those services, quality standards and performance against targets;*
> - *are provided with explanations about proposed service changes and have an opportunity to influence decisions on such changes;*
> - *are aware of the reasons for decisions and actions affecting their own treatment;*
> - *know what information is available and where they can get it.*
>
> (Code of Practice on Openness in the NHS, 1995)

It is worth noting that the Codes of Practice stated explicitly that they were not intended to provide access to actual documents or files, only to information from them. The Code of Practice on Access to Government Information states:

> *There is no commitment that pre-existing documents, as distinct from information, will be made available in response to requests . . . the Code should not be regarded as a means of access to original documents or personal files.*

The Codes are not legally enforceable. However, complaints about the failure to release information in line with the Codes' provisions can be made to the Ombudsman set up for the particular service (although this has to be undertaken through a Member of Parliament).

All the Codes contain various exemption provisions and reference to a public interest test. In the case of the Welsh Assembly Code the standard for the test for what is contrary to the public interest is higher than the other Codes. While all the Codes recognize the need for exemptions, there has been some difficulty in achieving a balance. It is generally accepted that the exemptions contained in the Government Code, for example, are very broad. This has meant that government departments and agencies have frequently been criticized for looking for opportunities to refuse requests for information.

One important piece of practical advice: the Codes of Practice and the Freedom of Information Act 2000 should be looked at together. Those organizations that have already taken on board the culture of the Codes will find implementation of the legislation much easier.

The Code of Practice on Access to Government Information

The Code of Practice came into effect on 4 April 1994 and included five commitments, to:

- supply facts and analysis of the facts which the government considers relevant and important in framing major policy proposals and decisions
- open up internal guidelines about government departments' dealings with the public
- supply reasons for administrative decisions
- provide information under the Citizen's Charter about public services, what they cost, targets, performance, complaints and redress
- respond to requests for information relating to policies, actions and decisions.

The National Assembly for Wales, Code of Practice on Public Access to Information

The Code of Practice issued by the National Assembly for Wales goes further than any other in providing rights of access to information. It is a reflection of the Assembly's desire to be at the forefront of promoting open government and included commitment to the following principles:

- maximizing openness in its business
- presenting National Assembly business in clear language, in line with its bilingual policy and taking account of different needs
- using the internet as a means of publishing National Assembly information

- maintaining a register of documents published by the National Assembly
- respecting personal privacy, commercial confidentiality, the duty of confidence and all laws governing the release of information
- providing a prompt and comprehensive response to requests for information (15 days is the time limit set by the Code)
- providing a right of complaint where a member of the public is not satisfied with the response received
- providing information free of charge where possible.

The Code of Practice on Openness in the NHS

The NHS Code builds on the progress made by the Patient's Charter (now super-seded by *Your Guide to the NHS*) which set out the rights of people to information about the NHS:

> *Because the NHS is a public service, it should be open about its activities and plans. So, information about how it is run, who is in charge and how it performs should be widely available. Greater sharing of information will also help foster mutual confidence between the NHS and the public.*

Information which must be provided under the NHS Code of Practice is set out in Table 1.3.

Table 1.3 Information provided under NHS Code of Practice

Type of information	NHS Trusts	District Health Authorities and Family Health Services Authorities	GPs, dentists, community pharmacists and optometrists	GP fundholders
Information about what services are provided, the targets and standards set and results achieved, and the costs and effectiveness of the service	Annual report; annual business plan summary; a summary strategic direction document, setting out plans for the delivery of services over a five-year period; audited accounts; information required under other codes (e.g. board members' private interests, performance tables)	Annual report, including a report by the Director of Health; annual report on performance against Patient's Charter rights and standards; audited accounts; a summary strategic direction document, setting out plans for the delivery of services over a five-year period; information required under other codes (e.g. board members' private interests, performance tables)		Annual practice plan; annual performance report; audited accounts

Continued on next page

Table 1.3 *Continued*

Type of information	NHS Trusts	District Health Authorities and Family Health Services Authorities	GPs, dentists, community pharmacists and optometrists	GP fundholders
Important proposals and decisions on health policies and on changes to delivery of services	Quarterly board reports; information on service changes; patient information leaflets	Annual purchasing plans; consultations with Community Health Councils		Plans for major shifts in purchasing
Information about the way in which health services are managed and provided, and who is responsible	Quarterly board reports; description of facilities; waiting times; clinical audit reports; information about clinicians (qualif-ications, areas of special interest, etc.); standing financial instructions; names and contact (office) numbers of board members and senior officers	List of GPs, dentists, pharmacists and optometrists; contracts with providers, both NHS and non-NHS; names and contact (office) numbers of Authority board members and senior officers	Practice leaflets – essential information about individual doctors' practices (e.g. qualifications, availability, clinic times, staff employed, services available, geographical boundary)	Practice leaflets – essential information about individual doctors' practices (e.g. qualifications, availability, clinic times, staff employed, services available, geographical boundary)
Information about how the organization communicates with the public	Agenda and papers relating to meetings (including a public meeting which must be held at least once a year); results of user surveys and action to be taken; volume and cat-egories of complaints and letters of appreciation, and performance in handling complaints	Papers, agendas and minutes of board meetings held in public [all board meetings must be held in public, although there are provisions for certain issues to be addressed in private]; Results of user surveys and action to be taken	Emergency arrangements; health promotion leaflets	Complaints procedures; health promotion leaflets
Information about how to contact Community Health Councils and the Health Service Commissioner	Patient information leaflets			

Continued on next page

Table 1.3	*Continued*			
Type of information	NHS Trusts	District Health Authorities and Family Health Services Authorities	GPs, dentists, community pharmacists and optometrists	GP fundholders
Information about how people can have access to their own personal health records	Patient information leaflets	Information leaflets	Patient information leaflets; copies of results of eye tests	

Further details can be obtained from the Code itself.

Manifestos and White Paper

Prior to the 1997 general election the Labour Party included in its manifesto a promise to introduce a 'Freedom of Information Act leading to more open government'. When it was elected to office it quickly published the White Paper *Your Right to Know*: *The Government's proposals for a Freedom of Information Act* (Cm 3818, December 1997). In a preface to the White Paper the Prime Minister, Tony Blair, said:

> *The Government is pledged to modernise British politics. We are committed to a comprehensive programme of constitutional reform. We believe it is right to decentralize power; to guarantee individual rights; to open up Government; and to reform Parliament. . . . .This White Paper explains our proposals for meeting another key pledge – to legislate for freedom of information, bringing about more open Government. The traditional culture of secrecy will only be broken down by giving people in the United Kingdom the legal right to know. This fundamental and vital change in the relationship between government and governed is at the heart of this White Paper.*

The Government published a draft Freedom of Information Bill for public consultation and pre-legislative scrutiny on 24 May 1999 (Cmnd 4355). The Freedom of Information Bill was introduced and had its First Reading in the House of Commons on 18 November 1999. The Second Reading debate was on 7 December 1999. Some concessions were made by the Government during the Commons report stage before the Bill was introduced in the Lords in April 2000, although it did not start its Committee stage until November 2000. Further minor amendments were made before the Bill became law on 1 December 2000.

Policy

When the Labour Party won the election of 1997 it set about delivering on the pledges set out in its manifesto of that year. David Clark became the Cabinet Office

minister in charge of delivering on the pledges. The Queen's Speech on 14 May prom-
ised a White Paper and a draft Bill on FOI. After the White Paper was published (in
December 1997), the Commons Select Committee on Public Administration published a report (HC 398) welcoming its proposals. The Government published its
response to the Committee on 21 July 1998 (HC 1020).

David Clark lost his post in the Government's first Cabinet reshuffle a few days
later and responsibility for FOI was transferred from the Cabinet Office to the Home
Office, enabling the policy to be developed alongside other constitutional measures, such as human rights and data protection.

In February 1999, while the draft Freedom of Information Bill was being prepared, the Home Secretary established the Advisory Group on Openness in the
Public Sector. The setting up of the Group was accompanied by recognition that
Government alone could not bring about the culture change necessary in public
sector bodies for a more open approach with the public. A substantial programme
of work was also needed to create the culture of openness. It was clear from experience overseas that this was as important as the legislation itself. The terms of
reference of the Group were:

- To advise the Home Secretary on proposals for promoting a cultural change in the public sector to foster a culture of greater openness
- To assist in the development of training and education programmes for public servants
  to promote cultural change and facilitate the introduction of Freedom of Information
- To undertake other tasks related to the implementation of Freedom of Information
  as directed by the Home Secretary.

After the 2001 general election it was announced on 8 June that the policy lead
on Freedom of Information and Data Protection was to be transferred from the
Home Office to the Lord Chancellor's Department (now the Department for Constitutional Affairs).

2

The legislation

This chapter describes the Freedom of Information Act 2000 in some detail, focusing on those areas which affect the practitioner's work – advice and assistance to users, implications of the right of access, the role of exemptions to the provision of information, use of the 'public interest' provision, costs and fees, publication schemes, and the Codes of Practice authorized by the Act. It provides an overview of these areas in a legislative context; succeeding chapters describe their implementation.

The Freedom of Information Act 2000 aims to strike a balance between extending people's access to official information and preserving confidentiality where disclosure would be against the public interest. The presumption, however, is that information is available unless it falls under a specified exemption. The scales are weighed in favour of openness.

The main features of the Act are:

- a general right of access to information held by public authorities
- exemptions from the duty to provide information
- a requirement on public authorities to exercise discretion; they may have to disclose information even when it may be exempt under the Act (the 'public interest test')
- arrangements in respect of costs and fees
- a duty on public authorities to adopt publication schemes
- arrangements for enforcement and appeal
- Codes of Practice.

One unique aspect of the Act (in United Kingdom legislation) is that it is wholly retrospective. It applies to all information held by public authorities regardless of its date. Like some other countries' enactments in this area, it does not apply only to information created or held by public authorities after it has come into force. This provision in the legislation has far-reaching effects, particularly in the way public authorities manage their information and records. This is explored more fully in Chapter 6. Some secondary legislation under the Act has already been passed and more is likely to follow (see Table 2.1).

Table 2.1 Secondary legislation under the Freedom of Information Act

Title	Reference	Content
The Freedom of Information Act 2000 (Commencement No 1) Order 2001	SI 2001 No 1637 (C 56)	Brings into force technical provisions of the Act
The Freedom of Information (Additional Public Authorities) Order 2002	SI 2002 No 2623	Adds further public authorities to the coverage of the Act
The Freedom of Information Act 2000 (Commencement No 2) Order 2002	SI 2002 No 2812	Brings into force the provisions which implement the first three stages of the FOI implementation timetable and places a duty on the bodies listed to comply with the publication scheme provisions of the Act (from 30 November 2002, 28 February 2003 and 30 June 2003 respectively for the bodies indicated)
The Freedom of Information (Excluded Welsh Authorities) Order 2002	SI 2002 No 2832	Excludes certain public authorities from the definition of 'Welsh public authority' for the purposes of the Act

Advice and assistance

Public authorities have a duty under the Act to provide advice and assistance to people who wish to make, or have made, requests for information. This may be interpreted in several different ways by public authorities (for example, by the provision of leaflets, a help line, or e-mail request facility) but the legislation does state that public authorities that conform to the Code of Practice under section 45 of the Act are deemed to have complied with the duty to provide advice and assistance.

Advice and assistance may involve advising the applicant that another person or agency may be able to help them with their application or, in exceptional circumstances, offering to take a note of the application over the telephone and sending a note to the applicant for confirmation (once confirmed and returned by the applicant, the note would constitute a written request and the time limit for reply would begin).

In practical terms it would be wise for public authorities to issue leaflets on using the provisions of the Act and generally to advertise how they deal with requests. Organizations should certainly consider issuing a leaflet with all responses to requests which states the applicant's rights regarding complaint, appeal, etc.

Right of access
Confirm or deny

> *Any person making a request for information to a public authority is entitled to be informed in writing by the public authority whether it holds information of the description specified in the request and, if that is the case, to have that information communicated to him.*

The provisions in this section of the Act (1(1)) are commonly referred to as 'the duty to confirm or deny that information is held, and to provide it'.

There are six reasons why a public authority may not have to meet this provision (these are examined in more detail in the following pages):

- where it is reasonable that further information is needed before the request can be answered (and the applicant has been so informed)
- an exemption applies
- the public interest in maintaining the exemption outweighs the public interest in disclosing the information
- when any fee is charged, and that fee is not paid within three months of a fees notice being issued
- if the public authority estimates that the cost of complying with the request would exceed the 'appropriate limit'
- if the request is vexatious or repeated.

A public authority may also not have to confirm or deny that it holds the requested information if Part II of the Act says so. This is the part which covers exempt information, and those exemptions in which this occurs are referred to in Chapter 3. Under some of these, certain conditions have to be met before the duty to confirm or deny is not applicable. Clearly the duty to confirm or deny does not arise when information is already accessible or when information is intended for future publication.

It is also worth noting that not all enquiries are necessarily FOI requests. An enquiry has to be a request for information as opposed to what might be termed a 'transactional request' – for example, a request to order a supply of a material or commodity; a request to attend a function.

Request for information

> *. . . a request for information is . . . a request which is in writing, states the name of the applicant and an address for correspondence, and describes the information requested.*

These are the three essentials that have to be met by anyone requesting information under the Act:

- put it in writing
- name and address
- description of the information requested.

A request must be treated as being in writing where the text of the request is transmitted by electronic means and is received in legible form. It should also be capable of being used for subsequent reference by the public authority.

Notice that the applicant does not have to mention the Act itself when making the request. Prior to implementing the Act fully on 1 January 2005 it would be good practice for public authorities if they started treating all enquiries as if they were requests under the Act. This would also give them an insight into the kinds of requests that will have to be dealt with in the legislative environment.

An applicant has to identify himself or herself for the purposes of the application but the identity of the applicant is otherwise of no concern to the public authority, except in the case of vexatious or repeated requests and personal information (if the applicant is the subject of the personal information, the provisions of the Data Protection Act 1998 will apply).

The applicant need not be a United Kingdom national or resident. A request for information can be made by any individual or body, anywhere in the world. There is also no restriction on the reasons why the information is being requested. Indeed the public authority cannot make enquiries as to why the information is being sought or what it will be used for.

The public authority can request any further information necessary from the applicant in order to identify and locate the information. There are no formal requirements on applicants to describe the information in a particular way (for example, they cannot be expected to quote references of particular documents or describe particular records) but the description has to be sufficient for a public authority to identify and locate the information requested. If a request is ambiguous an authority can seek reasonable clarification. There is no reason why communication with the applicant cannot be made by telephone, if that is possible.

The information communicated to the applicant has to be the information held at the time the request was received. Account may be taken of amendments or deletions that would have been made in the normal course of events.

The public authority must help the applicant to frame a request for information if they are not able to do so for themselves. They might, for example, take the request on the telephone, write it down and then confirm with the applicant that the contents of the request are accurate. Alternatively the public authority might refer the applicant to another source of help. Remember the duty to provide advice and assistance!

As soon as verification of the request is received, the 20-working-day deadline begins.

Form of reply

Where . . . the applicant expresses a preference for communication . . . namely –

- *. . . a copy of the information . . .*
- *. . . a reasonable opportunity to inspect a record containing the information*
- *. . . a digest or summary of the information . . .*

The public authority shall so far as reasonably practicable give effect to that preference.

If the applicant asks for the information in one of the three formats stated in the Act, the public authority should comply, if it is reasonable to do so. If the applicant does not express a preference, the authority may provide the information in any reasonable form. However, given the duty under the Act to provide advice and assistance (see page 10), the authority ought, in this situation, to be in a position to ask the applicant in which format they would like the information requested.

Cost may be taken into account in considering whether it would be reasonable to comply with the applicant's wishes. The public authority may decide that it is not reasonable to comply with such wishes, in which case it must inform the applicant of the reasons for the decision.

Time

. . . a public authority must comply . . . promptly and in any event not later than the twentieth working day following the date of receipt.

This provision is really at the heart of the Act. From it stems many of the important requirements in complying with the legislation, such as good records management, an infrastructure to handle requests quickly and efficiently, a system for logging requests, and training and awareness of authorities' staff.

In simple terms a clock starts ticking the moment a request is received. A public authority must confirm or deny that it has the information requested and provide it before the end of 20 working days from the date of receipt of the request. The 20-working-day limit applies irrespective of the geographical location of the applicant. The clock will stop only in the following circumstances:

- when a request for payment is sent to the applicant; it will start again (from where it stopped, not back to the beginning of the 20 days) when the appropriate fee is received
- when a request for information is transferred to another public authority (rather than stopping the clock, this is more the completion of the request as far as the original public authority is concerned, since it has to inform the applicant that the request has been transferred).

Note that where a public authority decides that it has to consult another authority, the clock does not stop.

Held (by a public authority)

. . . information is held by a public authority if –

- *it is held by the authority, otherwise than on behalf of another person, or*
- *it is held by another person on behalf of the authority.*

The Act does not talk about who created the information or who owns it, but about who *holds* it. Even if the information held is duplicated (and the original is held in another public authority), this does not obviate the authority's responsibility to confirm or deny that the information is held and to provide it in accordance with the requirements of the Act. It may need to consult another public authority about whether the information might be regarded as exempt, but such consultation will still fall within the 20-working-day deadline for response.

However, 'information held' does not extend to information held on behalf of another person or authority (for example, a Minister's private papers held in a government department, or where an authority is providing formal custody for another authority). It does extend to information held elsewhere on behalf of a public authority (for example, where records are held in a private storage facility).

Where a public authority does not hold all or some of the information relating to a request but believes that it is held by another public authority, then the authority must tell the applicant that it does not hold the information or part of it. However, if the public authority holds some of the information requested, it must tell the applicant what information it is holding (assuming it can be disclosed) before proceeding further with the request. The public authority might then do one of several things:

- tell the applicant that the rest of the information requested is held by another public authority or other public authorities
- refer the applicant to the other authority or authorities
- contact the other authority or authorities to confirm whether the information is indeed held there
- transfer the request
- if it is decided to transfer the request, ask the applicant if they object.

In deciding any of these actions the public authority must bear in mind the duty to provide advice and assistance (see page 10) and the ticking clock of the 20-working-day deadline.

Consultation

The Code of Practice under section 45 of the Act (see Appendix 1) makes it clear that where the consent of a third party would enable a disclosure to be made, a public authority should consult that third party prior to making a decision. This would be necessary where the disclosure of information would affect the legal rights of third parties. For example, provisions in the Data Protection Act 1998 and the Human Rights Act 1998 require that certain information be treated in confidence. However, where third-party legal rights are not affected, the public authority has an option to consult or not. For example, it would not be necessary to consult where there is other overriding legislation. It may also not be necessary to consult where the views of the third party would not affect the decision to disclose or withhold the information.

Consultation might be with one person or a representative group. If no response to consultation is received, the public authority is still bound by the requirements of the Act. It cannot, therefore, refuse a request simply because there has been no response to its consultation. Nor is the 20-working-day deadline extended for any consultation.

The section 45 Code of Practice does recommend two circumstances in which consultation should take place:

- where the views of the third party may assist the authority to determine whether the information requested is exempt from disclosure
- where the views of the third party may assist the authority to determine where the balance of the public interest lies.

It is for the public authority, not the third party, to determine whether or not information should be disclosed. If the third party does not consent to disclosure, that does not in itself mean that information must be withheld.

Vexatious or repeated request

If a request is considered vexatious by the public authority, it does not have to comply with it. Although it should be the authority's last resort to dismiss requests on these grounds, there may be no alternative. Where it is the case, the authority must tell the applicant in writing that the request is judged to be vexatious. This provision is not intended to include otherwise valid requests in which the applicant happens to take an opportunity to vent their frustration. A public authority is not expected to provide advice and assistance to applicants whose requests are vexatious.

A repeated request is one that is identical or substantially similar to an earlier satisfied request made by the same person and in which a reasonable interval of time has not elapsed. As with the vexatious request, the authority must tell the applicant in writing that the request is judged to be repeated.

Refusing a request

A request can be refused on five grounds, where:

- an exemption applies
- the public authority has asked for further information (see page 12)
- the request is vexatious
- the request is repeated
- the cost of complying exceeds the appropriate limit.

The Act requires a public authority to give the applicant notice of refusal to answer a request for information. This notice has to be given within the 20-working-day time limit for complying with requests.

In the case of exempt information the authority must specify the exemption or exemptions in question. The notice must state:

- the fact of the refusal
- the exemption in question
- why the exemption applies (if that is not otherwise apparent) but not if this would involve the disclosure of information which would itself be exempt.

When the public authority needs to apply the public interest test and has not yet reached a decision whether to confirm, deny, refuse or disclose, the notice must state that no decision has been reached and give an estimate of the date by which the public authority expects to make the decision. When, or if, a decision has been made, the notice must state that the public interest in maintaining the exemption or in not confirming or denying that the information is held outweighs the public interest in disclosing whether the public authority holds the information or in disclosing it. For more details on the application of the public interest test, see page 23.

All notices refusing a request must also contain or include:

- details of the right for applicants to apply to the Information Commissioner for a decision notice
- details of the authority's procedures for dealing with complaints about the handling of requests for information, or
- a statement that the public authority has no such complaints procedure.

This information might take the form of a general leaflet on handling FOI requests which includes the details for complaining and appealing against the Information Commissioner's decisions.

If the request is judged to be vexatious or repeated, the authority does not have to give the notice of refusal where such a notice has already been given and it is unreasonable to expect another to be issued.

The cost of complying with a request might include circumstances where a record (more usually one that has been archived) is not in a suitable condition to be copied or handled. This is usually termed 'unfit for production'. A public authority could undertake to repair the relevant documentation, providing the applicant with an estimate of the time taken to undertake the work. It may decide to include the cost of repair in its charges, in giving effect to any preference expressed by the applicant over the means of providing the information. Alternatively the public authority might decide that such a charge would not be reasonable under the Act. The authority might make the document available under supervision. Care has to be taken that exempt information, which may be part of the same document, is not inadvertently made available.

Exemptions

Under Freedom of Information there is a presumption of openness, irrespective of the date of the information, unless an exemption applies. The balance between being more transparent and open, and protecting information so that business can continue effectively was the subject of much debate during the framing of the legislation. It is bound to continue so. Maintaining the balance is not an easy process for public authorities. It is not surprising, therefore, that the application of the exemptions is a complex issue. Case law and good practice will continue to inform this area of the legislation for some time to come.

For public authorities outside central government there will be some exemptions which will not apply. These are the exemptions that are relevant only to the interests of the government as a whole and to the state, such as those relating to national security, international relations and defence.

It is generally accepted that there are 23 exemptions but a few of these cover more than one facet. There are two categories of exemptions:

- public interest – those in which the public authority seeking to rely on the exemption has to establish that the public interest in maintaining the exemption outweighs the public interest in disclosing the information
- absolute – where no public interest test is required.

Some exemptions automatically cease to apply after a pre-defined period. In the case of those exemptions without such a period, the information remains exempt for as long as the criteria for the exemption last.

Table 2.2 describes the exemptions. It arranges them in class or prejudice categories:

- class – where the exemption relates solely to the type of information
- prejudice – where a test of prejudice needs to be applied.

Chapter 3 examines the exemptions in more detail and provides guidance on their implementation.

Table 2.2 Exemptions from the duty to provide information

Exemption	Description	Absolute or public interest	Section of the Act and duration
1. Class:			
Already accessible	Reasonably accessible to the applicant by other means (such as by virtue of other legislation or in a publication scheme), even if only on payment. For example: • certificates of birth, marriage and death (available under other legislation) • books, pamphlets and leaflets (published)	Absolute	21 30 years
Intended for future publication	Information intended for publication where it is reasonable that it should not be disclosed until the intended date of publication. Normally the publication scheme will cover this; where it does not, authorities must tell the applicant when publication is planned. For example: • minutes and papers of regular (e.g. monthly) meetings • results of research projects	Public interest	22 30 years

Supplied by, or relating to, bodies dealing with security matters	The following bodies are specified:
	• Security Service
	• Secret Intelligence Service
	• Government Communications Headquarters (GCHQ)
	• Special Forces
	• tribunals established under:
	  — s.65 Regulation of Investigatory Powers Act 2000
	  — s.7 Interception of Communications Act 1985
	  — s.5 Security Service Act 1989
	  — s.9 Intelligence Services Act 1994
	• Security Vetting Appeals Panel
	• Security Commission
		Absolute	23
			No specified limit

Continued on next page

Table 2.2 *Continued*

Exemption	Description	Absolute or public interest	Section of the Act and duration
	• National Criminal Intelligence Service • Service Authority for the National Criminal Intelligence Service		
International relations (1)	Confidential information obtained from a state other than the UK or from an international organization or international court	Public interest	27 No specified limit
Investigations and proceedings conducted by public authorities	Information held by a public authority for the purposes of a criminal investigation or criminal proceedings, or information obtained from confidential sources by the public authority for the purposes of criminal investigations, criminal proceedings, other specified investigations, or civil proceedings arising from such investigations	Public interest	30 30 years (but no specified limit for information relating to civil proceedings which use confidential sources)
Court records	Information contained in: • any document filed with a court for the purpose of proceedings in a particular cause or matter • any document served on, or by, a public authority for the purposes of proceedings in a particular cause or matter • any document created by a court or member of the administrative staff of a court for the purpose of proceedings in a particular cause or matter • any document placed in the custody of a person conducting an enquiry or arbitration for the purposes of that enquiry or arbitration Any document created by a person conducting an enquiry or arbitration for the purposes of that enquiry or arbitration	Absolute	32 30 years
Formulation of Government policy	Information relating to: • formulation or development of Government policy • ministerial communications • request for and provision of advice by law officers • operation of ministerial private offices	Public interest	35 30 years
Communications with Her Majesty or about honours	Information relating to communications with the royal family or royal household or to the conferring of any honour or dignity by the Crown	Public interest	37 30 years (royal family etc.) 60 years (honours)

Continued on next page

Table 2.2 *Continued*

Exemption	Description	Absolute or public interest	Section of the Act and duration
Environmental information	Information relating to the environment as defined in the Environment Information Regulations (EIR) 2003	Public interest	39 No specified limit
Personal information (1)	Information which constitutes 'personal data' as defined by the Data Protection Act 1998. This may be data which relates to the applicant (the data subject) – in which case it is covered by the Data Protection Act	Absolute	40 Lifetime of the data subject
Commercial interests (1)	Trade secrets	Public interest	43 30 years
Prohibitions on disclosure	• prohibited by or under any enactment • incompatible with any European Community obligation • would constitute or be punishable as a contempt of court	Absolute	44 No specified limit
2. Prejudice: National security	Information required for the purpose of safeguarding national security	Public interest	24 No specified limit
Defence	If the information would, or would be likely to, prejudice the defence of the British Islands or of any colony, or the capability, effectiveness or security of the armed forces of the Crown and any forces co-operating with those forces	Public Interest	26 No specified limit
International relations (2)	If the information would, or would be likely to, prejudice: • relations between the UK and any other state • relations between the UK and any international organization or international court • interests of the UK abroad • promotion or protection by the UK of its interests abroad	Public interest	27 No specified limit
Relations within the United Kingdom	If the information would, or would be likely to, prejudice relations between any two administrations in the UK (i.e. Government of the United Kingdom, Scottish Administration, Executive Committee of the Northern Ireland Assembly, National Assembly for Wales)	Public interest	28 30 years

Continued on next page

Table 2.2 *Continued*

Exemption	Description	Absolute or public interest	Section of the Act and duration
The economy	If the information would, or would be likely to, prejudice the economic interests of the UK or the financial interests of any administration in the UK	Public Interest	29 No specified limit
Law enforcement	If the information would, or would be likely to, prejudice: • prevention or detection of crime • apprehension or prosecution of offenders • administration of justice • assessment or collection of any tax or duty or any imposition of a similar nature • operation of immigration controls • maintenance of good security and good order in prisons or other institutions where people are lawfully detained • civil proceedings brought by or on behalf of the public authority • exercise of public authority functions for: — ascertaining whether any person has failed to comply with the law — ascertaining whether anyone is responsible for any conduct which is improper — ascertaining whether circumstances exist or may exist which would justify regulatory action — ascertaining whether a person is fit or competent in relation to the management of corporate bodies — ascertaining the cause of an accident — protecting charities against misconduct or mismanagement — securing the health, safety and welfare of persons at work	Public interest	31 100 years
Audit functions	If the information would, or would be likely to, prejudice the audit of public accounts or the examination of the economy, efficiency and effectiveness with which public authorities use their resources in discharging their functions	Public interest	33 30 years

Continued on next page

Table 2.2 *Continued*

Exemption	Description	Absolute or public interest	Section of the Act and duration
Parliamentary privilege	Information required for the purpose of avoiding an infringement of the privileges of the Houses of Parliament	Absolute	34 No specified period
Prejudice to effective conduct of public affairs	Including information which would, or would be likely to, prejudice: • maintenance of the convention of the collective responsibility of Ministers • work of the Executive Committee of the Northern Ireland Assembly • work of the executive committee of the National Assembly for Wales Or would, or would be likely to, inhibit: • free and frank provision of advice • free and frank exchange of views for the purpose of deliberation	Public interest, except for information held by the Houses of Parliament (which is absolute)	36 30 years
Health and safety	Information which would, or would be likely to, endanger the physical or mental health or the safety of any individual	Public interest	38 No specified period
Personal information (2)	Information which constitutes 'personal data' as defined by the Data Protection Act 1998 (DPA). This may be data which relates to an identifiable individual other than the applicant, and: • disclosure would contravene any of the data protection principles • the person to whom it relates would not have a right to know about it or a right of access to it under the DPA • disclosure would affect an individual's right to prevent processing that might cause damage or distress under the DPA	Absolute	40 Lifetime of the data subject
Information provided in confidence	Information obtained from any other person the disclosure of which would constitute a breach of confidence actionable by any person	Absolute	41 No specified period
Legal professional privilege	Information in respect of which a claim to legal professional privilege (in Scotland to confidentiality of communications) can be maintained	Public interest	42 30 years
Commercial interests (2)	Information which would, or would be likely to, prejudice the commercial interests of any person	Public interest	43 30 years

Public interest

> *... the public interest in maintaining the exclusion of the duty to confirm or deny outweighs the public interest in disclosing whether the public authority holds the information ...*
>
> *... If ... the public interest in maintaining the exemption outweighs the public interest in disclosing the information.*

When a request for information is received and the public authority decides that an exemption applies to some or all of the information requested, there are six instances when this is the end of the matter (except where the applicant might appeal against non-disclosure). These are the six absolute exemptions:

- already accessible
- supplied by, or relating to, bodies dealing with security matters
- court records
- parliamentary privilege
- information provided in confidence
- prohibitions on disclosure.

In addition, two other exemptions are partly absolute:

- personal information
- prejudice to the effective conduct of public affairs (information held by the Houses of Parliament).

The rest of the exemptions are subject to the public interest test – where the public authority needs to balance the public interest in withholding the information against the public interest in making it available. This task does not fall within the 20-working-day deadline but public authorities are expected to inform applicants of the likely date for decision and to take that decision within a reasonable time.

The 'public interest' is not defined by the Act. A case-by-case assessment will be required. This is the first aspect of the Act that is likely to be tested in law and it will no doubt be a prominent subject in the related case law. Among the aspects that will have to be taken into consideration are:

- the amount of damage to a particular interest (the greater such damage, the greater the weight of public interest there will have to be)
- timing (for example, releasing information before a trial may well prejudice the outcome of the proceedings)
- the importance of openness and transparency (for example, the expenditure of public funds)
- the public's need to be better informed (for example, so that they can better participate in public affairs or be more aware of any danger to public health)
- reasons for decisions.

If it would involve the disclosure of information which would itself be exempt information, a public authority does not have to state why an exemption applies, having applied the public interest test, or why it has decided not to disclose or to refuse to confirm or deny.

Costs and fees

The Act does not require public authorities to make charges for providing information but they have discretion to do so. There are limits and conditions.

The Secretary of State (for Constitutional Affairs) will make regulations for the charging of fees. These regulations do not apply to:

• information which is already reasonably accessible (as in the exemption described on page 18)
• material available under a publication scheme
• disclosure of information for which a charge can be made under any other enactment.

The regulations will cover four main areas:

• definitions
• the appropriate limit
• maximum fees
• aggregation of requests.

Definitions

• disbursements – any costs directly and reasonably incurred by a public authority:
  — in informing the applicant whether it holds information of the description specified in the request, and
  — in communicating such information to the applicant
• prescribed costs – any costs reasonably incurred by a public authority:
  — in determining whether it holds information of the description specified in the request
  — in locating and retrieving any such information, and
  — in giving effect to any preference expressed by the applicant as to the means of communication of the information.

Note that the cost of staff time incurred in determining whether the public authority is obliged to comply with the request (for example, consultation with another body; does an exemption apply?) is not included in either of these definitions and therefore cannot be charged for.

The appropriate limit

The limit is defined in section 12 of the Act ('such amount as may be prescribed, and different amounts may be prescribed in relation to different cases') and is currently set at £550. This figure will change in line with agreed changes to the figure set for the disproportionate cost of answering parliamentary questions. A public authority is not obliged to comply with a request for information if it estimates that the cost of doing so would exceed the appropriate limit (although it can do so if it wishes).

Maximum fees

The costs to be taken into account by public authorities when calculating fees are the prescribed costs:

- Where the sum of these costs exceeds the appropriate limit, the public authority may charge a fee of:
  — 10 per cent of the prescribed costs for the first £550 of such costs
  — all of the prescribed costs for such costs over £550
  — the disbursements.
- Where the sum of these costs does not exceed the appropriate limit, the public authority may charge a fee of:
  — 10 per cent of the prescribed costs
  — the disbursements.

Aggregation of requests

Under certain circumstances a public authority can aggregate two or more requests in determining whether the cost of complying with the requests would exceed the appropriate limit. These circumstances are:

- the requests are for information which is on the same subject matter or is otherwise related
- the last of the requests is received by the public authority before the twentieth working day following the date of receipt of the first of the requests
- the public authority judges that the requests have been made in an attempt to ensure that the prescribed costs of complying separately with each request would not exceed the appropriate limit.

Example 1

Request for a health and safety report and minutes of a meeting to discuss the issues [*specified*] covered by the report, together with related correspondence

Time spent looking for the report and related records:
   9 hours @ £12 per hour
   = £108.00
Photocopying of papers, 120 sheets @ 10p per sheet
   = £12.00

Fee:10% of £108.00	=	£10.80
	+	£12.00
	Total	£22.80

Example 2

Request for copies of papers relating to an investigation into building problems for a [*specified development*], including meetings, reports, project documents [*specified*].

Time spent looking for and retrieving information:
   120 hours @ £11 per hour
   = £1,320.00
Photocopying of reports, 80 pages @ 10p per page
   = £8.00

Fee:10% of £550.00	=	£ 55.00
+ remaining prescribed costs	=	£770.00
	+	£ 8.00
Total		£833.00

The regulations will also allow the public authority to charge for any additional disbursements involved in providing the information. For example, the applicant may ask for the information to be supplied in a language other than English. These costs will fall outside the appropriate limit.

If for any reason the applicant is not prepared to pay the fees notified in any fees notice, the public authority should consider whether there is any information in which the applicant might be interested and which is available free of charge. Where the request exceeds the appropriate limit and the public authority is not prepared to use its discretionary powers in this respect, it should consider informing the applicant what information can be provided within the limit.

Both these procedures fall within the authority's duty to provide advice and assistance.

There may be occasions when a fee is paid by the applicant and the public authority subsequently finds that the information requested falls under one or more exemptions. At the time of writing the Department for Constitutional Affairs is examining this issue, to decide whether a fee, or part of it, is still chargeable or not.

Publication schemes

A central plank of the Act is the section relating to publication schemes. These embody the Government's push for transparency and openness. Given the link between schemes and the section of the Act (21) relating to information already accessible being exempt, it is in the interests of public authorities to use them as extensively as possible to publish information. Their greater use will save time and money by not having to answer individual requests, and will provide a more proactive service to the public.

Publication schemes are schedules of classes of information which authorities will publish as a matter of course. The schedules must contain:

- the classes of information which are or will be published
- the manner in which the material is published (including a contact point if the material is to be sent to the applicant)
- what charge, if any, will be made for supply of the material.

Charges made for the supply of material included in a publication scheme are not part of the fees regulations described on page 24. The authority may charge what it deems reasonable.

Publication schemes have to be approved by the Information Commissioner. A public authority is free to produce its own scheme, suited to its own circumstances. However, the Act provides for model publication schemes in respect of public authorities falling within particular classes. These schemes are designed to be used by a number of public authorities carrying out similar functions. For example, hospital trusts in the National Health Service, universities, primary schools, or parts of local government. The Information Commissioner has approved several such model schemes. These can be found on the Commissioner's website: www.informationcommissioner.gov.uk.

Public authorities may adopt a model publication scheme as it stands, or may introduce modifications to tailor it to their particular requirements. If any such modifications are made, the Information Commissioner's approval is required.

Approval of publication schemes has been a phased exercise, in advance of full implementation of the Act in January 2005. Table 2.3 shows the dates by which publication schemes for different parts of the public sector have to be approved by the Information Commissioner. The Commissioner has asked that draft schemes be submitted to him at least three months before the approval dates.

Table 2.3 Timetable for approval of publication schemes

Public authorities	Approval date
Central government departments (except the Crown Prosecution Service and the Serious Fraud Office) Parliament National Assembly for Wales Non-departmental public bodies subject to the jurisdiction of the Parliamentary Ombudsman	30 November 2002
Local government (except police authorities)	28 February 2003
Police Police authorities Crown Prosecution Service Serious Fraud Office Armed Forces	30 June 2003
National Health Service	31 October 2003
Schools Universities Publicly owned companies Remaining non-departmental public bodies	29 February 2004
Remaining public authorities	30 June 2004

The Act allows public authorities to publish their publication schemes in such manner as they think fit. Many have used, and will use, the internet to publish their schemes. This will, in most cases, be the most convenient method but authorities must consider those with special needs, including those without access to the internet. There is no obligation under the Act to provide translations of information published in a scheme or to provide the information in a different medium. Public authorities should note, however, that they may be subject to other legislation in this area, such as the Race Relations Act 1976, the Welsh Language Act 1993, the Disability Discrimination Act 1995 or the Northern Ireland Act 1998.

Commitments that were made by central government departments and non-departmental public bodies in accordance with the Code of Practice on Access to Government Information, that is:

- information on what public services are provided
- how public services are run
- how much public services cost
- who is in charge of providing public services
- complaints and redress procedures available to the public
- what targets are set
- what standards of service are expected
- results achieved

have to be carried forward to the publication schemes.

In addition, guidance issued by the Lord Chancellor's Department to central government departments and agencies in 2002 suggests that the following information should also be included:

- mission, objectives and functions of the organization
- structure of the organization
- who is responsible for what function, and how they can be contacted
- minutes and papers of management board meetings (these could be a summary of proceedings where confidential information might still need to be protected)
- financial information in addition to regular accounts, such as income – how it is raised and spent
- internal guidance to officials.

Guidance similar to that issued to central government organizations was also issued by the Lord Chancellor's Department to local authorities. Bearing in mind that local authorities have been required to publish information as a result of the Local Government (Access to Information) Act 1985 and guidance issued by the Association of County Councils, Association of District Councils and Association of Metropolitan Councils in 1995 (*Open Government – A Good Practice Note on Access to Information*), this suggests that the following information should also be available in publication schemes:

- background to the publication scheme
- rights of access generally available to the citizen
- structure of the authority
- explanation of how the classes of information are compiled
- details of how to access the information
- how information is generally published by the authority
- decision-making process of the authority
- information which will need to be requested separately because of its unique nature or sensitivity
- archived information
- specific advice for citizens who are unable to access information in the normal way
- frequently requested information
- complaints procedure
- how the scheme will be reviewed
- index to the scheme.

Detailed guidance on the implementation of publication schemes can be found in Chapter 4.

Codes of Practice

The Act provides for two Codes of Practice to be issued (and revised as necessary). These cover:

- the discharge of public authorities' functions under the Act
- the keeping, management and destruction of records.

These codes are not statutory Codes of Practice but, of course, they derive their authority from the Act. The point is made in the Codes that a failure to comply may lead to a failure to comply with the Act or indeed with other legislation (such as the Disability Discrimination Act 1995, the Public Records Act 1958 and the Local Government (Access to Information) Act 1985).

The Information Commissioner has a duty to promote observance of the Codes by public authorities and accordingly, if it appears to him that an authority is not complying with one of the Codes, he may issue a practice recommendation, specifying the steps which should be taken to promote compliance. The practice recommendation has to be given in writing and has to specify those parts of the Code(s) with which the authority is not complying. Failure to comply with a practice recommendation may lead to an adverse comment in the Information Commissioner's report to Parliament.

Both Codes of Practice have been in force since 30 November 2002. However, most of the provisions in them relate to the provisions of Part I of the Act, which does not come into force until 1 January 2005. Guidance on the provisions of the Codes is contained elsewhere in this publication under the appropriate subject heading. Both Codes are reproduced in full in Appendix 1. The following is a summary of the Codes' contents:

Access Code – section 45

One of the most important roles of the section 45 Code of Practice is that, in complying with it, public authorities will have been deemed to have met the duty under the Act of providing advice and assistance.

The aims of this Code of Practice are to:

- facilitate the disclosure of information under the act by setting out good administrative practice for public authorities to follow when handling requests for information
- protect the interests of applicants by setting out standards for the provision of advice and by encouraging the development of effective means of complaining about decisions taken under the Act
- ensure that the interests of third parties who may be affected by the disclosure of information are considered

- ensure that authorities consider FOI before agreeing to confidentiality clauses in contracts and to the confidentiality of information from a third party.

The main features of this Code of Practice are:

- provision of advice and assistance to persons making requests for information
- handling requests for information which appear to be part of an organized campaign
- timeliness in dealing with requests for information
- charging fees
- transferring requests for information
- consultation with third parties
- public sector contracts
- accepting information in confidence from third parties
- consultation with devolved administrations
- refusal of request
- complaints procedure.

Records Management Code – Section 46

This Code makes the very important observation:

Any freedom of information legislation is only as good as the quality of the records to which it provides access. Such rights are of little use if reliable records are not created in the first place, if they cannot be found when needed or if the arrangements for their eventual archiving or destruction are inadequate.

This echoes the statements made in the White Paper *Your Right to Know* (Cm 3818) which kick-started the legislation.

While the Code covers all public authorities, it also outlines special best practice and recommendations for authorities subject to the Public Records Acts 1958 and 1967 (mainly central government bodies).

The Code is a great opportunity for all public authorities. For very many years the status of the records management function has suffered greatly. It has been starved of resources and has not received the organizational support to make an effective contribution to business operations. This Code sets out clearly the steps to achieving the effective management of an authority's records and information. Its high-level profile, linked as it is to major legislation, should enable authority information managers to wield it in such a manner that those resources and that support which have been sadly lacking are forthcoming.

The main features of Part One of this Code of Practice are:

- the records management function
- policy statements
- human resources
- management of active records
  — record creation
  — record keeping
  — record maintenance
- disposal arrangements
  — record closure
  — appraisal planning and documentation
  — record selection
- management of electronic records.

Part Two covers the review and transfer of public records (as defined by Schedule 1 of the Public Records Act 1958) and an annex provides a selective list of standards used in records management.

Chapter 6 examines the Code of Practice in detail and looks at the practical steps that need to be taken to introduce an effective records management programme.

Enforcement and appeal

It shall be the duty of the Commissioner to promote the following of good practice by public authorities and . . . to promote the observance by public authorities of –

(a) the requirements of this Act, and
(b) the provisions of the codes of practice under sections 45 and 46.

Under the Act the Data Protection Commissioner became known as the Information Commissioner, and the Data Protection Tribunal as the Information Tribunal. The new post of Information Commissioner came into being on 30 January 2001. Thus the same person, and office, has responsibilities under the Data Protection Act 1998 and the Freedom of Information Act 2000. This (and the relationship with other legislation) is examined in Chapter 7.

In relation to the Freedom of Information Act the duties of the Information Commissioner are to:

- promote the observance by public authorities of good practice
- provide information to the public about how the Act works and about good practice under the Act
- lay before Parliament an annual report on the exercise of the Commissioner's functions under the Act
- consult with others about public records:

— the Keeper of Public Records about promotion of the Records Management Code of Practice in relation to public records as defined by Schedule 1 of the Public Records Act 1958

— the Deputy Keeper of the Records of Northern Ireland (now called the Chief Executive) about promotion of those provisions relating to public records of Northern Ireland, as defined in the Public Records Act (Northern Ireland) 1923.

The Information Commissioner is also responsible for arranging the dissemination of information about the operation of the Act. In this respect much has been published on the Commissioner's website: www.informationcommissioner.gov.uk.

The Commissioner's powers may be summarized as to:

- approve and revoke publication schemes
- provide advice about the Act
- assess whether a public authority is following good practice
- charge fees for services provided (subject to the agreement of the Secretary of State)
- issue practice recommendations
- serve:
  — decision notices – where an applicant can apply for a decision from the Information Commissioner whether a request for information has been dealt with in accordance with the provisions of Part I of the Act
  — information notices – where the Information Commissioner requires further information in order to determine whether a public authority has complied with the provisions of Part I of the Act or the Codes of Practice
  — enforcement notices – where the Information Commissioner is satisfied that a public authority has failed to comply with the provisions of Part I of the Act, and serves a notice requiring the authority to take steps to comply
- enter and inspect public authority premises, in accordance with Schedule 3 of the Act
- prosecute any offence under the Act.

Complaints and appeals

Applicants for information have three courses of complaint or appeal:

- They can complain to the public authority about the operation of the Act (for example, the lack of advice or assistance, or the refusal to provide information in the form requested). The authority's existing complaints procedure should be used to handle these actions. Where no such procedure is in place, the person in the organization deciding on or judging the complaint must be someone more senior than the person who made the original decision about which the applicant is complaining.

- They can appeal to the Information Commissioner about the refusal to provide information.
- They can appeal to the Information Tribunal about a decision made by the Information Commissioner.

Any further appeal can only be brought (to a court) on a point of law.

The complaints procedure to follow under the Act is set out in the Access Code of Practice under section 45 of the Act. Its main features are:

- A complaints procedure must be in place by the date that a public authority's publication scheme comes into effect.
- From 1 January 2005 the complaints procedure will also be required to deal with complaints relating to the general right of access.
- When answering a request for information public authorities should provide details of their complaints procedures and inform the applicant of the right to appeal to the Information Commissioner if they are dissatisfied with the authority's decision.
- Review of decisions taken in accordance with the Act should include those about where the public interest lies in respect of exempt information.
- Review should be handled by a person who was not party to the original decision.
- Complaints should be acknowledged and the complainant informed of the likely date for determining the complaint.
- Public authorities should publish their target times for dealing with complaints.

Detailed procedures on enforcement and ways in which appeals against decisions under the Act can be made are described in Chapter 5.

3

Exemptions

Under Freedom of Information there is a presumption of openness, irrespective of the date of the record, unless an exemption applies. The exemptions are set out in Part II of the Act. This chapter examines the exemptions in detail, providing examples of how the process might be put into practice. The numbers after the headings are the sections in the Act, and an indication of whether the exemption is absolute or subject to the public interest test is also made. The duration of the exemption is shown at the end of each section.

Information accessible to applicant by other means (section 21) – absolute

Information which is reasonably accessible to the applicant otherwise than under section 1 is exempt information.

A public authority has a duty to confirm or deny that it holds information in this category but not to provide it. It should inform the applicant where the information can be obtained (for example, it may be accessed through the authority's publication scheme). If it does not, it may lay itself open to a complaint that it is not providing advice and assistance as required by section 16 of the Act.

It is important to take regard of the word 'reasonably'. Information may still be reasonably accessible even if it involves the payment of a fee. However, since the Act says reasonably accessible *to the applicant*, account should be taken of the applicant's financial resources. Information may thus be reasonably accessible to a large company but not to one individual.

Also, in the case where information is made available for inspection in one place only (whether this is in accordance with a statutory obligation or not) and the applicant lives a considerable distance from that place, it could be argued that the information is not reasonably accessible. This would not apply, of course, if the applicant can be supplied with a copy of the relevant information.

It is also likely to be seen as unreasonable if the applicant states a preference to see the information and then argues that it is unreasonable for them to travel to see it. Such an instance should not arise because access to the information will be stated where it is made available (for example, in a publication scheme).

An applicant may also argue that information is not reasonably accessible if it is available only in digital form. In such cases a public authority should make arrangements for a printed copy to be provided. For the time being it is unlikely that an applicant could successfully argue that information is not reasonably accessible if it is not available in digital form.

In archive establishments, if catalogues are available in a reading room or on a website, the request can be directed that way. This interpretation will help archives to prioritize their cataloguing projects – focusing on those uncatalogued collections that are likely to be the subject of FOI requests. Note, however, that the National Archives (formerly the Public Record Office) and the Public Record Office of Northern Ireland cannot claim this exemption.

Section 21 example

A local authority will already have in place arrangements for publishing reports in accordance with the Local Government (Access to Information) Act 1985. An application for this information under FOI will be declared exempt and dealt with under those arrangements, referring the applicant accordingly.

Annual reports are almost universally likely to appear in publication schemes. An applicant for such a report will be referred to the appropriate scheme.

Duration

30 years

Information intended for publication (section 22) – public interest

Information is exempt information if –

(a) *the information is held by the public authority with a view to its publication, by the authority or any other person, at some future date (whether determined or not),*

(b) *the information was already held with a view to publication at the time when the request for information was made*

(c) *it is reasonable in all the circumstances that the information should be withheld from disclosure until the date referred to in paragraph (a).*

The duty to confirm or deny does not apply if compliance with that duty would involve the disclosure of information covered by this exemption.

It is unlikely that information held back as a result of administrative inefficiency or to cover official embarrassment will fall under this exemption. However, many public authorities are likely to use this category to manage the release of their information. For example, where parties to a particular issue need to be informed first (as might be the case in a police investigation).

Again, the use of the word 'reasonable' is important in this exemption. Future case law may well be a determinant here but any delay longer than a year may well be considered unreasonable.

Section 22 example

If a public authority has undertaken to include minutes and papers of its Management Board in its publication scheme, those for a particular meeting may not be published until they are ratified at the next meeting. This may be monthly, quarterly or, exceptionally, annually.

Duration

30 years

Information supplied by, or relating to, bodies dealing with security matters (section 23) – absolute[1]

Information held by a public authority is exempt information if it was directly or indirectly supplied to the public authority by, or relates to, any of the bodies specified . . .

The bodies referred to by this exemption are:

* Security Service (MI5)
* Secret Intelligence Service (MI6)
* Government Communications Headquarters (GCHQ) – including any part of the armed forces of the Crown which is for the time being required by the Secretary of State to assist GCHQ in carrying out its functions
* Special Forces (such as the SAS)
* Tribunals established under:
  — s.65 Regulation of Investigatory Powers Act 2000
  — s.7 Interception of Communications Act 1985
  — s.5 Security Service Act 1989
  — s.9 Intelligence Services Act 1994
* Security Vetting Appeals Panel
* Security Commission
* National Criminal Intelligence Service
* Service Authority for the National Criminal Intelligence Service.

These bodies are not public authorities under the Act so information cannot be sought directly from them. This exemption relates to information from or relating to the bodies which is held by another public authority.

The duty to confirm or deny does not apply if compliance with that duty would involve the disclosure of information covered by this exemption.

Evidence that specified information was directly or indirectly supplied by, or relates to, any of the bodies covered by this exemption can be certified by a Minister of the Crown. An appeal against the issue of such a certificate can be made to the Information Tribunal.

Duration

No specified limit

National security (section 24) – public interest

Information which does not fall within section 23(1) [as above] *is exempt information if exemption from section 1(1)(b) is required for the purpose of safeguarding national security.*

The duty to confirm or deny does not apply if compliance with that duty would involve the disclosure of information covered by this exemption.

This exemption is largely self-explanatory but public authorities should bear in mind that a simple assertion that information is being withheld because of national security is likely to be challenged.

Section 24 example

A public authority that holds information relating to safety precautions at a nuclear establishment may assert that such information is exempt under this provision.

Duration

No specified limit

Defence (section 26) – public interest

Information is exempt information if its disclosure under this Act would, or would be likely to, prejudice –

(a)   the defence of the British Islands or of any colony, or

(b)   the capability, effectiveness or security of any relevant forces.

The duty to confirm or deny does not apply if compliance with that duty would involve the disclosure of information covered by this exemption.

This exemption is also largely self-explanatory. It is worth noting that 'relevant forces' does not include the Special Forces and parts of the armed forces required to assist GCHQ in their work which are not subject to the Act (see page 37).

Section 26 example

Information relating to combat readiness or capabilities of the armed forces is likely to be exempt.

Duration

No specified limit

International relations (section 27) – public interest

Information is exempt information if its disclosure under this Act would, or would be likely to, prejudice –

(a) *relations between the United Kingdom and any other State,*
(b) *relations between the United Kingdom and any international organisation or international court,*
(c) *the interests of the United Kingdom abroad, or*
(d) *the promotion or protection by the United Kingdom of its interests abroad.*

The duty to confirm or deny does not apply if compliance with that duty would involve the disclosure of information covered by this exemption.

In addition to the quoted subsection of the Act this exemption also includes confidential information obtained from a State other than the United Kingdom or from an international organization or international court.

Duration

No specified limit

Relations within the United Kingdom (section 28) – public interest

Information is exempt information if its disclosure under this Act would, or would be likely to, prejudice relations between any administration in the United Kingdom and any other such administration.

The duty to confirm or deny does not apply if compliance with that duty would involve the disclosure of information covered by this exemption.

'Administration in the United Kingdom' is defined to include:

- the government of the United Kingdom
- the Scottish Administration
- the Executive Committee of the Northern Ireland Assembly
- the National Assembly for Wales.

Duration

30 years

The economy (section 29) – public interest

Information is exempt information if its disclosure under this Act would, or would be likely to, prejudice –

(a) the economic interests of the United Kingdom or of any part of the United Kingdom, or

(b) the financial interests of any administration in the United Kingdom as defined by section 28(2).

The duty to confirm or deny does not apply if compliance with that duty would involve the disclosure of information covered by this exemption.

As above, 'Administration in the United Kingdom' is defined to include:

- the government of the United Kingdom
- the Scottish Administration
- the Executive Committee of the Northern Ireland Assembly
- the National Assembly for Wales.

Section 29 example

The premature disclosure of the intentions of the government contained in its budget (for example, taxation) would fall under this exemption.

Duration

No specified limit.

Investigations and proceedings conducted by public authorities (section 30) – public interest

(1) *Information held by a public authority is exempt information if it has at any time been held by the authority for the purposes of –*

(a) *any investigation which the public authority has a duty to conduct with a view to it being ascertained –*

(i) *whether a person should be charged with an offence, or*

(ii) *whether a person charged with an offence is guilty of it.*

(b) *any investigation which is conducted by the authority and in the circumstances may lead to a decision by the authority to institute criminal proceedings which the authority has power to conduct, or*

(c) *any criminal proceedings which the authority has power to conduct.*

(2) *Information held by a public authority is exempt information if –*

(a) *it was obtained or recorded by the authority for the purposes of its functions relating to –*

(i) *investigations falling within subsection (1)(a) or (b)*

(ii) *criminal proceedings which the authority has power to conduct,*

(iii) *investigations (other than investigations falling within subsection (1)(a) or (b)) which are conducted by the authority for any of the purposes specified in section 31(2) and either by virtue of Her Majesty's prerogative or by virtue of powers conferred by or under any enactment, or*

(iv) *civil proceedings which are brought by or on behalf of the authority and arise out of such investigations, and*

(b) *it relates to the obtaining of information from confidential sources.*

The duty to confirm or deny does not apply if compliance with that duty would involve the disclosure of information covered by this exemption.

The exemption covers information held at any time and therefore will cover such information even where an investigation has been completed. It is likely that the public interest test will be brought to bear on this particular exemption more than most of the others, since there will be considerable pressure for information relating to the investigation into disasters such as Hillsborough, the *Marchioness* and Paddington to be released.

Note that the exemption has two distinct parts:

• information held for the purposes of criminal investigations and proceedings
• information obtained from confidential sources.

Duration

30 years (first part)
No specified limit (second part)

Law enforcement (section 31) – public interest

Information which is not exempt information by virtue of section 30 is exempt information if its disclosure under this Act would, or would be likely to, prejudice –

(a) *the prevention or detection of crime*

(b) *the apprehension or prosecution of offenders*

(c) *the administration of justice*

(d) *the assessment or collection of any tax or duty or of any imposition of a similar nature*

(e) *the operation of the immigration controls*

(f) *the maintenance of security and good order in prisons or in other institutions where persons are lawfully detained*

(g) *the exercise by any public authority of its functions for any of the purposes specified in subsection (2)*

(h) *any civil proceedings which are brought by or on behalf of a public authority and arise out of an investigation conducted, for any of the purposes specified in subsection (2), by or on behalf of the authority by virtue of Her Majesty's prerogative or by virtue of powers conferred by or under an enactment, or*

(i) *any inquiry held under the Fatal Accidents and Sudden Deaths Inquiries (Scotland) Act 1976 to the extent that the inquiry arises out of an investigation conducted, for any of the purposes specified in subsection (2), by or on behalf of the authority by virtue of Her Majesty's prerogative or by virtue of powers conferred by or under an enactment.*

The duty to confirm or deny does not apply if compliance with that duty would involve the disclosure of information covered by this exemption.

The purposes that are referred to in the subsection cover a wide range of law enforcement functions:

- ascertaining whether any person has failed to comply with the law
- ascertaining whether any person is responsible for any conduct which is improper
- ascertaining whether circumstances which would justify regulatory action in pursuance of any enactment exist or may arise
- ascertaining a person's fitness or competence in relation to the management of bodies corporate or in relation to any profession or other activity which they are, or seek to become, authorized to carry on
- ascertaining the cause of an accident
- protecting charities against misconduct or mismanagement (whether by trustees or other persons) in their administration
- protecting the property of charities from loss or misapplication
- recovering the property of charities
- securing the health, safety and welfare of persons at work

- protecting persons other than persons at work against risk to health or safety arising out of or in connection with the actions of persons at work.

Section 31 example

The disclosure of the registration numbers of unmarked police cars could prejudice the prevention or detection of crime.

Duration

100 years

Court records (section 32) – absolute

(1) *Information held by a public authority is exempt information if it is held only by virtue of being contained in –*

    (a) *any document filed with, or otherwise placed in the custody of, a court for the purposes of proceedings in a particular cause or matter,*

    (b) *any document served upon, or by, a public authority for the purposes of proceedings in a particular cause or matter, or*

    (c) *any document created by –*

       (i) *a court, or*

       (ii) *a member of the administrative staff of a court,*

       for the purposes of proceedings in a particular cause or matter.

(2) *Information held by a public authority is exempt information if it is held only by virtue of being contained in –*

    (a) *any document placed in the custody of a person conducting an inquiry or arbitration, for the purposes of the inquiry or arbitration, or*

    (b) *any document created by a person conducting an inquiry or arbitration, for the purposes of the inquiry or arbitration.*

The duty to confirm or deny does not apply if compliance with that duty would involve the disclosure of information covered by this exemption.

This exemption applies only to information held by public bodies other than the courts and tribunals, which are not themselves public authorities under the Act. The exclusion of the courts and tribunals from the Act was deliberate so that the disclosure of information on law enforcement is still governed by these legal bodies.

The exemption relates to particular causes or matters. Other general information relating to law enforcement and court proceedings would not fall under the exemption (for example, statistics relating to the number of offences).

Duration

> 30 years

Audit functions (section 33) – public interest

> *Information held by a public authority to which this section applies is exempt informa-*
> *tion if its disclosure would, or would be likely to, prejudice the exercise of any of the*
> *authority's functions in relation to any of the matters referred to in subsection (1).*

The duty to confirm or deny does not apply if compliance with that duty would involve the disclosure of information covered by this exemption.

This section applies only to those public authorities which:

- audit the accounts of other public authorities
- examine the economy, efficiency and effectiveness with which other public authorities use their resources in discharging their functions.

This means that internal audit information would not fall under this exemption.

Those public authorities which are covered by this section include the National Audit Office and the Audit Commission.

Duration

> 30 years

Parliamentary privilege (section 34) – absolute

> *Information is exempt information if exemption from section 1(1)(b) is required for the*
> *purpose of avoiding an infringement of the privileges of either House of Parliament.*

The duty to confirm or deny does not apply if compliance with that duty would involve the disclosure of information covered by this exemption.

Evidence that specified information needs to be covered by this exemption can be certified by the Speaker of the House of Commons (in relation to the privileges of the House of Commons) or the Clerk of the Parliaments (in relation to the privileges of the House of Lords). An appeal against the issue of such a certificate is not possible.

Section 34 example

Information held by a public authority which comprises private discussions of a Select Committee of Parliament would be covered by this exemption.

Duration

No specified limit

Formulation of Government policy (section 35) – public interest

Information held by a Government department or by the National Assembly for Wales is exempt information if it relates to –

(a) *the formulation or development of government policy,*
(b) *Ministerial communications,*
(c) *the provision of advice by any of the Law Officers or any request for the provision of such advice, or*
(d) *the operation of any Ministerial private office.*

The duty to confirm or deny does not apply if compliance with that duty would involve the disclosure of information covered by this exemption.

Note that the exemption covers the 'formulation or development' of Government policy not its execution or the attendant procedures and administrative functions.

When Government policy has been finalized, any statistical information used as part of the process of reaching the policy decision will not be covered by this exemption. The public interest test is likely to be brought into play where there is any doubt about what kind of information constitutes statistics.

Duration

30 years

Prejudice to effective conduct of public affairs (section 36) – public interest[2]

Information to which this section applies is exempt information if, in the reasonable opinion of a qualified person, disclosure of the information under this Act –

(a) *would, or would be likely to, prejudice –*
   (i) *the maintenance of the convention of the collective responsibility of Ministers of the Crown, or*
   (ii) *the work of the Executive Committee of the Northern Ireland Assembly, or*
   (iii) *the work of the executive committee of the National Assembly for Wales,*
(b) *would, or would be likely to, inhibit –*
   (i) *the free and frank provision of advice, or*
   (ii) *the free and frank exchange of views for the purposes of deliberation, or*

(c) would otherwise prejudice, or would be likely otherwise to prejudice, the effective conduct of public affairs.

The duty to confirm or deny does not apply if compliance with that duty would involve the disclosure of information covered by this exemption.

Since this is a class-based exemption (with the exception of information held by the House of Commons and the House of Lords), the public authority will need to demonstrate that the specified prejudice will arise if it were to accept a request for information. In cases of doubt the authority can, as set out in this section, rely on the 'reasonable opinion of a qualified person' (with the exception of statistical information, in which case it has to provide the evidence itself). 'Qualified person' means:

- in relation to information held by a government department in the charge of a Minister of the Crown – any Minister of the Crown
- in relation to information held by a Northern Ireland department – the Northern Ireland Minister in charge of the department
- in relation to information held by any other government department – the commissioners or other person in charge of that department
- in relation to information held by the House of Commons – the Speaker of the House of Commons
- in relation to information held by the House of Lords – the Clerk of the Parliaments
- in relation to information held by the Northern Ireland Assembly – the Presiding Officer
- in relation to information held by the National Assembly for Wales – the Assembly First Secretary
- in relation to information held by any Welsh public authority other than the Auditor-General for Wales – the public authority or any officer or employee of the authority authorized by the Assembly First Secretary
- in relation to information held by the National Audit Office – the Comptroller and Auditor-General
- in relation to information held by the Northern Ireland Audit Office – the Comptroller and Auditor-General for Northern Ireland
- in relation to information held by the Auditor-General for Wales – the Auditor-General for Wales
- in relation to information held by any Northern Ireland public authority other than the Northern Ireland Audit Office – the public authority or any officer or employee of the authority authorized by the First Minister and deputy First Minister in Northern Ireland acting jointly
- in relation to information held by the Greater London Authority – the Mayor of London

- in relation to information held by a functional body within the meaning of the Greater London Authority Act 1999 – the chairperson of that functional body
- in relation to information held by any public authority not falling within the above – a Minister of the Crown, the public authority (if authorized for the purposes of this section of the Act by a Minister of the Crown) or any officer or employee of the public authority who is authorized for the purposes of this section of the Act by a Minister of the Crown.

Duration

30 years

Communications with Her Majesty, etc. and honours (section 37) – public interest

Information is exempt information if it relates to –

(a) communications with Her Majesty, with other members of the Royal Family or with the Royal Household, or

(b) the conferring by the Crown of any honour or dignity.

The duty to confirm or deny does not apply if compliance with that duty would involve the disclosure of information covered by this exemption.

This exemption will therefore cover letters and other documents received from the royal family and royal household and notes of meetings between representatives of public authorities and the royal family and household.

Duration

30 years (communications with Her Majesty, etc.)
60 years (honours)

Health and safety (section 38) – public interest

Information is exempt information if its disclosure under this Act would, or would be likely to –

(a) endanger the physical or mental health of any individual, or

(b) endanger the safety of any individual.

The duty to confirm or deny does not apply if compliance with that duty would involve the disclosure of information covered by this exemption.

This level of testing, 'endanger the physical or mental health', replaces the test of 'substantial distress' that has been common in access management regimes until now.

Duration

No specified limit

Environmental information (section 39) – public interest

Information is exempt information if the public authority holding it –

(a) *is obliged by regulations under section 74 to make the information available to the public in accordance with the regulations, or*

(b) *would be so obliged but for any exemption contained in the regulations.*

The duty to confirm or deny does not apply if compliance with that duty would involve the disclosure of information covered by this exemption.

Section 74 covers access to information under the Environmental Information Regulations (EIR). This is examined more closely in Chapter 7.

Duration

No specified limit

Personal information (section 40) – absolute[3]

(1) *Any information to which a request for information relates is exempt information if it constitutes personal data of which the applicant is the data subject.*

(2) *Any information to which a request for information relates is also exempt information if –*

(a) *it constitutes personal data which do not fall within subsection (1), and*

(b) *either the first or second condition . . . is satisfied.*

The duty to confirm or deny does not apply if compliance with that duty would involve the disclosure of information covered by this exemption. A data subject, however, has the right under the Data Protection Act 1998 to know whether personal data on them is being processed.

The conditions referred to in subsection (2) above are:

• where information falls within the definition of data in the Data Protection Act 1998, its disclosure otherwise than under the Act would contravene:

— any of the data protection principles
— the right to prevent processing likely to cause damage or distress[4]
where in any other case disclosure of the information otherwise than under the Act would contravene any of the Data Protection principles if the exemptions in section 33A of the Data Protection Act 1998 were disregarded
- by virtue of any provision of Part IV of the Data Protection Act 1998 the information is exempt from section 7(1)(c) of that Act (data subject's right of access to personal data).

Where an application to a public authority for personal data is made by the data subject of that data, that application needs to be handled according to the Data Protection Act 1998 rather than to this exemption.

Section 40 example

Thus if a person were to write to their local district council requesting access to the records of the housing department which has information on them, this exemption will apply, but the council will need to process the application in accordance with the provisions of the Data Protection Act 1998. Unless an exemption under the Data Protection Act applies, the person can see those records. The applicant does not have to specify that the request is being made under any particular enactment.

Where an application to a public authority for personal data is made by a person other than the data subject, that application needs to be handled according to the Freedom of Information Act 2000.

In most cases the release of personal data to third parties without consent will breach the Data Protection principles. This rather complicated part of the Act is examined more closely in Chapter 7.

At the time of writing the Office of the Information Commissioner has produced the very useful *Awareness Guidance on Personal Information*. This is available on their website: www.informationcommissioner.gov.uk.

Duration

Lifetime of the data subject

Information provided in confidence (section 41) – absolute

Information is exempt information if –

(a) it was obtained by the public authority from any other person (including another public authority) and

(b) *the disclosure of the information to the public (otherwise than under this Act) by the
public authority holding it would constitute a breach of confidence actionable by that
or any other person.*

The duty to confirm or deny does not apply if compliance with that duty would
involve the disclosure of information covered by this exemption.

Note that this exemption does not cover the public authority's own information which it might consider confidential but information in confidence received
from another person or authority. The authority's own confidential information will
likely fall under one of the other exemptions.

The important element here is whether disclosure of the information would constitute an actionable offence. Reams of paper have been written on this complex
question but there need to be three constituents:

- quality of confidence – the information must have this confidential nature
- obligation of confidence – the circumstances in which the information has
  been passed on must oblige the recipient to regard it as confidential
- unauthorized use – the confidential information has been used without the author-
  ization of the person passing it on and that has resulted in their detriment.

The Code of Practice under section 45 of the Act gives specific guidance on public sector contracts, and this includes advice to resist confidentiality clauses.

Section 41 example

If a contractor has contracted to provide facility management services to a public
authority and provides that public authority with information concerning its financial affairs in confidence, this exemption would apply.

At the time of writing the Office of the Information Commissioner has produced
the very useful *Awareness Guidance on Information Provided in Confidence*. This
is available on their website: www.informationcommissioner.gov.uk.

Duration

No specified limit

Legal professional privilege (section 42) – public interest

*Information in respect of which a claim to legal professional privilege or, in Scotland, to
confidentiality of communications could be maintained in legal proceedings is exempt information.*

The duty to confirm or deny does not apply if compliance with that duty would involve the disclosure of information covered by this exemption.

Law books and papers make a distinction between two types of legal professional privilege:

- legal privilege – communications between a client and a professional legal adviser for the purpose of giving or obtaining advice
- litigation privilege – all communications where these relate mainly to litigation.

Duration

30 years

Commercial interests (section 43) – public interest

Information is exempt information if it constitutes a trade secret [and] . . . if its disclosure under this Act would, or would be likely to, prejudice the commercial interests of any person (including the public authority holding it).

The duty to confirm or deny does not apply if compliance with that duty would involve the disclosure of information covered by the second part of this exemption (but not the first part, i.e. trade secrets).

'Trade secret' was defined by the House of Lords Select Committee which examined the draft freedom of information legislation in 1998 as: 'information of commercial value which is protected by the law of confidence'. There appears to be no other generally accepted definition.

The operation of case law will greatly help in the application of this particular exemption. Public authorities may find problems citing the exemption where, for example, the disclosure of information revealing mismanagement might, in the authority's opinion, prejudice their commercial interests.

Duration

30 years

Prohibitions on disclosure (section 44) – absolute

Information is exempt information if its disclosure (otherwise than under this Act) by the public authority holding it –

(a) is prohibited by or under any enactment,
(b) is incompatible with any Community obligation, or
(c) would constitute or be punishable as a contempt of court.

The duty to confirm or deny does not apply if compliance with that duty would involve the disclosure of information covered by this exemption.

There are some enactments under which public authorities have discretion to disclose information or not. These discretionary provisions are not covered by this exemption.

The Department for Constitutional Affairs is, at the time of writing, undertaking a review of statutory prohibitions on disclosure to see whether their retention is necessary. The Secretary of State has powers to repeal such Acts (section 75 of the Freedom of Information Act).

Note that the exemption also covers information which is prohibited from disclosure by European Community directives and regulations or by court orders.

Duration

No specified limit

General issues

Guidance on particular exemptions is expected from the Office of the Information Commissioner during 2004. In the meantime, here are some general questions/situations that may arise:

- Are earlier drafts releasable under FOI even when they contain material that did not end up as policy/procedures or that is sensitive?
  — Yes, these are possibly releasable. Sensitive information can be redacted, if necessary. Earlier drafts cannot be withheld if they, or any part of them, contain no exempt information. It is the information not the document or records which is being assessed under FOI.
  — Public authorities will need to look more closely at version control of documents and perhaps making it clear to applicants that certain records are drafts.
- Is a breach of confidence actionable when the person is not alive?
  — This may be so in certain circumstances. At the time of writing the Office of the Information Commissioner is producing guidance on information given in confidence. In most cases legal advice will need to be sought.
- How should exempt information be dealt with in a Publication Scheme?
  — Entire classes of information may have to be left out of a scheme because a proportion of the information covered is, or might be, exempt information. However, public authorities are encouraged to allow reference to a class of information notwithstanding that part of such information might be exempt, provided that reference to the use of a particular exemption is made clear when defining the class.

- When is a request for information vexatious?
  - In the context of a court action, an action is deemed to be frivolous and vexatious if it is one 'which no reasonable person could possibly treat as bona fide, and contend that he had a grievance which he was entitled to bring before the court.'[5]
  - A request will not be vexatious just because it is difficult to see why the applicant would want the information requested, or because considerable effort is required to retrieve the information.
  - A public authority wishing to decline a request on this basis must have reason to believe that the sole purpose of the applicant making the request is to cause annoyance or distress to the public authority, and to put it to trouble.
- How do you weigh up the balance of the public interest?
  - Guidance from the Information Commissioner is expected in 2004. Document the reasons for both sides as objectively as possible. The use of case law is likely to figure strongly in this area. Judging the public interest has happened in other countries, for example in Ireland in 1999:
    - Expenses paid to members of the Irish Parliament: the public interest in ensuring accountability for the use of public funds greatly outweighed any right to privacy in relation to details of expense claims;
    - The public interest in terms of openness and accountability of disclosing tender prices outweighed the possible harm to tenderers.

Notes

1   Unless in an historical record in the National Archives or the Public Record Office of Northern Ireland.
2   Except information held by either House of Parliament.
3   Part of the exemption is subject to the public interest test, see note 4.
4   Section 10 of the Data Protection Act; this is the qualified element of the exemption (i.e. subject to the public interest test).
5   Norman v. Matthews (1916) LJKB 857.

4

Publication schemes

This chapter gives advice on the structure and content of publication schemes, and highlights some of the procedures that practitioners will need to be aware of in maintaining schemes. It also provides some examples of current publication schemes.

A publication scheme is a guide to information which public authorities publish or intend to publish. It should focus on what will be of interest to the public, not necessarily what the public authority wants to include in the scheme. However, it is good to bear in mind that the more information included in publication schemes the less time will be spent by authorities in dealing with individual requests (and thus there will be a better service to the public).

Structure

A typical publication scheme will include the following:

- introduction
  - what the publication scheme is
  - contact name, telephone number and address of the person responsible for administering the scheme
  - objectives and functions of the organization[1]
  - organization of the public authority[2]
- classes of information
- manner in which the information is published
- charge (if any) for the provision of the information.

Publication schemes are promises. An authority is promising that all information relating to a particular class will be made public. Thus, if it says that minutes of a particular meeting will be published (without any condition attached), it will be expected that the minutes in their entirety will be made available. The public authority will not be able to rely on an exemption to withhold information which it has said in its publication scheme that it will publish.

Public authorities must also ensure that the necessary mechanisms are in place to meet the promises made in the schemes. Thus, specific material has to be identified, located and provided (which may involve sending in the post). Where information in the publication schemes is made available electronically, any necessary links have to be maintained and provision made for those who do not have access to the internet or who have special needs.

Public authorities should look upon publication schemes as a way of managing the release of all information whether it contains good news or bad news. Those implementing the scheme should therefore work closely with press and public relations staff.

Introduction

The introduction might also include the name and address of the person who can be contacted about access rights under the Data Protection Act and encourage feedback from the public on the operation of the scheme. The public will be more likely to use the scheme (and thus save numerous enquiries about its operation) if it is set out in straightforward and simple terms. Users of the scheme are consulting it to acquire information; their priority is not to find out the organization of the authority or become immersed in unnecessary detail, most of which is usually available elsewhere in a different context. Keep the introduction simple.

Public authorities should bear in mind that not all possible applicants for information will have access to the internet. The introduction might therefore highlight this point and give alternative advice to such people.

Classes of information

Information published by public authorities might be classified into broad categories, for example:

- corporate information (strategies, business plans, etc.)
- management information (policies)
- administrative information (procedures)
- operational information (results, statistics, outcomes, etc.).

Alternatively the scheme could be structured according to a public authority's organizational or function structure, for example:

Corporate information:

- annual reports
- planning and strategy
- estate management
  — London
  — Bootle
  — Sheffield
  — area offices
- statistics
- open government
- health and safety
- diversity in action programme (see Figure 4.1).

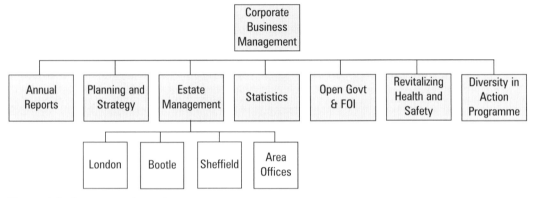

Figure 4.1 Corporate information

Communications

- liaison
- publicity
- parliamentary business (see Figure 4.2).

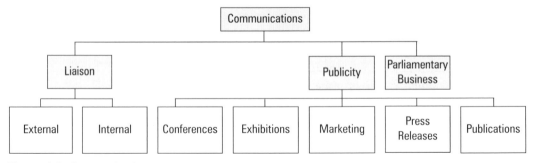

Figure 4.2 Communications

Whatever the structure used, the public authority must bear in mind the users of the scheme. A complicated structure will not make it easy for the public to locate information; similarly too broad a structure will not help an enquirer to pin down the information being sought. From the authority's point of view, a detailed breakdown may lead to frequent revision of the scheme.

Classes of information should not be confused with the actual information falling into a class. Such information may vary from time to time whereas the definition of a class will not change.

Manner in which information is published

The scheme should state how the information described can be obtained. This might be via the authority's website, in the form of a leaflet or standard publication (such as an annual report), a copy of relevant documentation or documentation available to inspect. Some information may be available in more than one form. The manner in which it is provided may require the applicant to telephone or write in to the public authority, in which case the appropriate details must be provided in the scheme against the class of information and (especially with telephone facilities) the appropriate response mechanisms must be in place.

Information may be available in different formats or in different documents. It must be routinely available as described in the publication scheme and this might therefore not be as easy as first thought. For example, it may be that some documents containing information described in the publication scheme also contain information that is exempt or that the public authority does not wish to include in the scheme. It is important, therefore, that systems for responding to the publication scheme are comprehensive and fully tested.

Charges

The charging regime for information provided through a publication scheme is separate from that for information provided as a result of individual requests (see page 24). A public authority can make any charge it considers reasonable for information from a publication scheme or it may not charge at all for some information. While the Act does not require a schedule of charges to be included in the publication scheme, an authority should state the charge(s) clearly for each class of information. An alternative might be to state simply that information is available free or on payment (the minimum required by the Act) and point the applicant to a separate price list elsewhere or include such a list with the scheme. Whatever steps are taken, the public authority should bear in mind the statutory duty to provide advice and assistance. It is in the interests of both parties to make the scheme simple and easy to use.

A public authority should continue to use its current charging systems to operate the publication scheme. This might involve sending out an invoice before supplying the information or providing the information with an invoice.

Guidance

At the time of writing most publication schemes will have been approved by the Information Commissioner and will be available. The guidance issued by the Office of the Information Commissioner (*Publication Schemes: Guidance and Methodology*, April 2003) will, however, still provide valuable advice for populating schemes and for their continued maintenance. Particular practical advice includes:

- The log of requests for information which does not form part of the publication scheme (see page 144) will enable the public authority to identify popular subjects and to consider whether the classes of information in the scheme might be added to.
- Public authorities need to identify key members of staff to implement the publication scheme – they may, for example, be shown in the scheme as points of contact for obtaining information. A scheme co-ordinator solely allocated to the task of implementing the publication scheme has proved an effective instrument in pilot schemes that were set up in central government departments.
- If a scheme is provided via the internet, it is advisable to ensure the involvement of technical staff so that the scheme is readily and consistently available.
- Key groups in the organization should be involved in running the scheme, such as:
  — legal teams
  — marketing staff
  — public consultation fora.

Approval criteria

The Information Commissioner's approval criteria for publication schemes are based upon the Act (sections 19 and 20). These include consideration as to whether the public authority has had regard:

- to the public interest in allowing public access to information held by the public authority
- in the publication of reasons for any decisions made by the public authority.

If the Information Commissioner refuses to approve a publication scheme, a statement of the reasons for doing so must be provided by the Commissioner. When approving a scheme, the Information Commissioner may state that the approval is to expire at the end of a specified period. The first set of approvals, as shown in the Table 2.3 on page 28, will expire four years after the relevant implementation date. Approved schemes may be revoked by the Information Commissioner, in which case the Commissioner is required to give six months' notice of such action.

Content

An essential part of the preparations for implementing FOI is for authorities to know what information they hold. With this knowledge publication schemes can be populated (and individual requests answered, and records managed effectively). A public authority may need to carry out an information survey or records audit in order to compile a comprehensive picture of the information they hold. Detailed guidance on undertaking an audit is in Chapter 6.

When setting up a publication scheme for the first time, the starting point has to be the information that a public authority already publishes (including that under any statute). Consideration can then be given to what additional information can be published, bearing in mind the approval criteria above. In the first wave of publication schemes the following types of information have figured strongly:

- corporate strategies and business plans
- work programmes
- minutes of regular meetings
- policies and procedures
- reports commissioned by authorities as a basis for decision making.

Public authorities may wish to consider the following kinds of information for inclusion in their schemes:

- guidance to staff
- background to policy
- management information
- public consultation
- circulars and notices
- decisions
- speeches (by ministers, chief executives, etc.)
- legislation and related information (although it is helpful to know that Her Majesty's Stationery Office in the Cabinet Office has responsibility for the publication of UK legislation; these feature in the HMSO publication scheme and can be viewed on its website: www.legislation.hmso.gov.uk.
- procurement, grants, loans, etc.
- information required to be published under other legislation
- research reports.

The following should also be borne in mind when deciding what to make available in publication schemes:

- exemptions – where no potential exemption exists, the information is more likely to be included in a scheme

- interest – where frequent requests for information of a particular sort have been received in the past, authorities should be more inclined to include it in a publication scheme
- data protection – information is exempt from disclosure if it would mean a breach of the data protection principles in the Data Protection Act 1998. This may mean that certain classes of information cannot be included in publication schemes. However, it may be possible for the public authority to define the class of information in its publication scheme in such a way that it excludes personal data; for example, minutes of management board meetings excluding information which identifies, or allows the identification of, individual members of staff
- a general copyright statement should be included in the scheme.

Adding and removing information

The review of a publication scheme or the merger of one organization with another or some such similar change may result in the need to add or remove classes of information from a publication scheme before it is due for reapproval. In this instance the public authority will need to submit the class to be amended to the Information Commissioner who will consider the application under the same criteria as applied to the original scheme. The resulting approved publication scheme will be the scheme as amended. The date for expiry of approval of the amended scheme will remain the original date.

Notification to the Information Commissioner is not required for the removal or addition of information falling within a class. Such information is very likely to change from time to time; for example, minutes of a committee which has ceased to exist.

Timing

There is no requirement under the Act to specify a time within which information from a publication scheme should be provided but public authorities will be expected to do so within a reasonable time. There may be some items of information whose release will depend on other factors. For example, facts and their analysis relating to policy decisions will normally be made available when policies and decisions are announced; papers relating to meetings may need to be made available weeks or months before or after the event; allowance should be made for the time taken to approve minutes of meetings.

Public authorities should consider for which formal meetings it is appropriate to publish the agenda, papers and minutes or summaries of these documents. Regular formal committees or advisory groups are more likely to be included than ad hoc or informal discussions.

Examples of schemes

National Archives

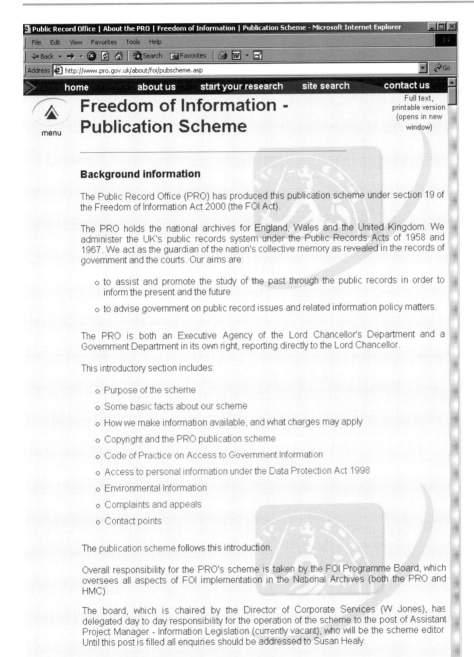

The image shows a Microsoft Internet Explorer browser window with the title bar "Public Record Office | About the PRO | Freedom of Information | Publication Scheme - Microsoft Internet Explorer". The address bar shows http://www.pro.gov.uk/about/foi/pubscheme.asp. The navigation bar includes: home, about us, start your research, site search, contact us. The page content reads:

Freedom of Information - Publication Scheme

Full text, printable version (opens in new window)

menu

Background information

The Public Record Office (PRO) has produced this publication scheme under section 19 of the Freedom of Information Act 2000 (the FOI Act).

The PRO holds the national archives for England, Wales and the United Kingdom. We administer the UK's public records system under the Public Records Acts of 1958 and 1967. We act as the guardian of the nation's collective memory as revealed in the records of government and the courts. Our aims are:

- o to assist and promote the study of the past through the public records in order to inform the present and the future
- o to advise government on public record issues and related information policy matters.

The PRO is both an Executive Agency of the Lord Chancellor's Department and a Government Department in its own right, reporting directly to the Lord Chancellor.

This introductory section includes:

- o Purpose of the scheme
- o Some basic facts about our scheme
- o How we make information available, and what charges may apply
- o Copyright and the PRO publication scheme
- o Code of Practice on Access to Government Information
- o Access to personal information under the Data Protection Act 1998
- o Environmental Information
- o Complaints and appeals
- o Contact points

The publication scheme follows this introduction.

Overall responsibility for the PRO's scheme is taken by the FOI Programme Board, which oversees all aspects of FOI implementation in the National Archives (both the PRO and HMC).

The board, which is chaired by the Director of Corporate Services (W Jones), has delegated day to day responsibility for the operation of the scheme to the post of Assistant Project Manager - Information Legislation (currently vacant), who will be the scheme editor. Until this post is filled all enquiries should be addressed to Susan Healy.

The PRO welcomes your feedback on this scheme.

West Berkshire Council

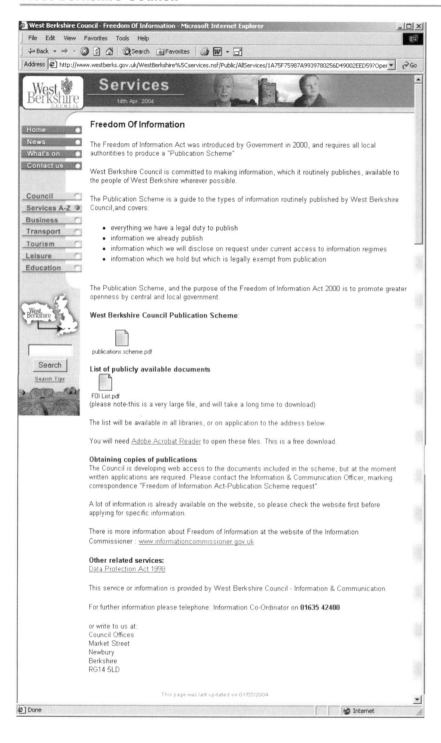

Aylesbury Vale District Council

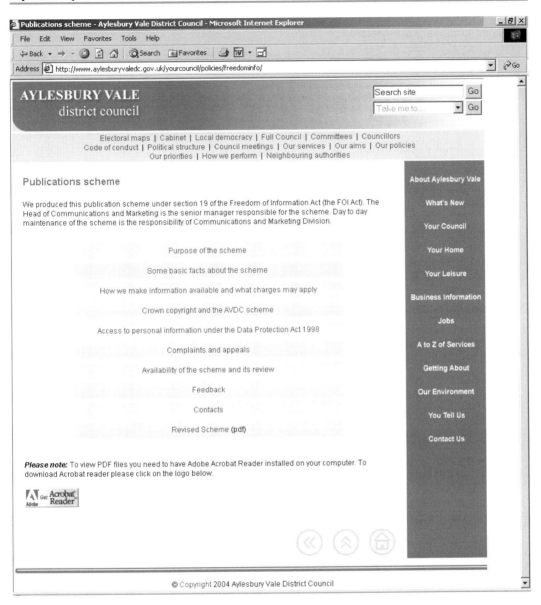

Gloucestershire Hospital NHS Trust

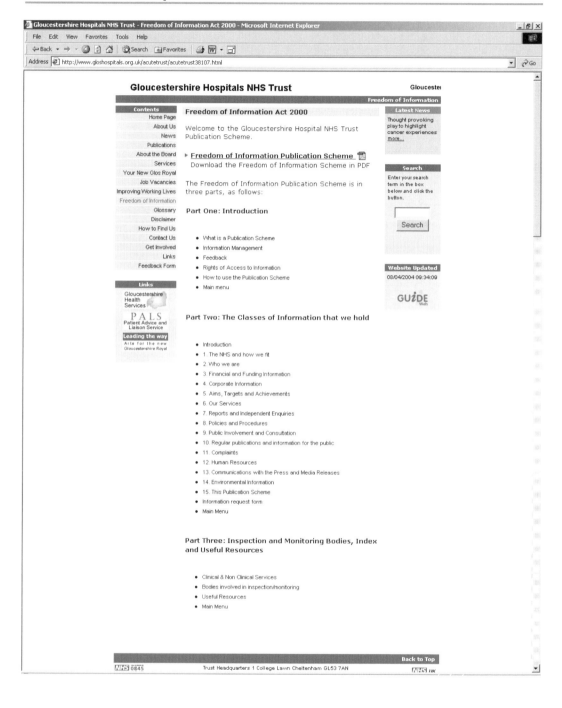

Essex Police Authority

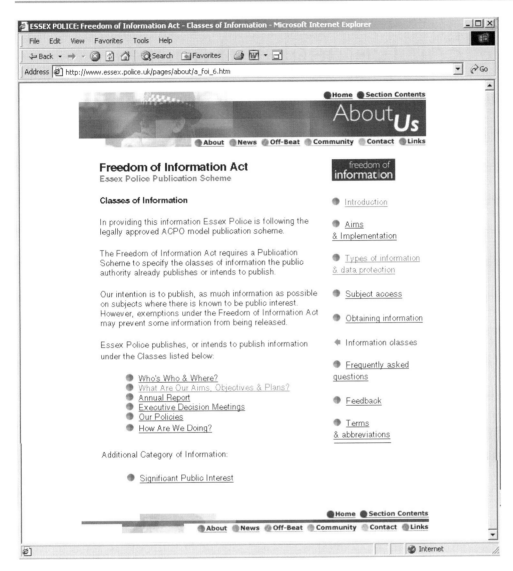

Notes

1   There is no need to duplicate this information if it is reasonably available elsewhere (for example, on the organization's website).

2   See note 1.

3   Renamed the National Archives on 2 April 2003.

5

Enforcement and appeal

This chapter describes how the Act is enforced by the Information Commissioner and how the procedure for appeals works.

The Information Commissioner enforces the Act largely through the issue of notices:

- practice recommendations
- decision notices
- information notices
- enforcement notices.

Practice recommendations

If it is brought to the Information Commissioner's notice that a public authority is not complying with either of the Codes of Practice provided for by the Act, the Commissioner may issue a practice recommendation to that authority. The practice recommendation must be given in writing and must include a reference to those provisions of the Code(s) with which the public authority is not complying, including the steps which must be taken in order to comply.

If the practice recommendation is issued (other than to the National Archives – formerly the Public Record Office) under the Records Management Code of Practice and relates to public records (as defined by Schedule 1 of the Public Records Act 1958), the Information Commissioner is required to consult the Keeper of Public Records or (other than to the Public Record Office of Northern Ireland) in the case of public records in Northern Ireland (as defined in the Public Records Act (Northern Ireland) 1923) the Deputy Keeper of the Records of Northern Ireland (now the Chief Executive).

A practice recommendation is simply a recommendation. It cannot be directly enforced by the Information Commissioner but failure to comply may mean a failure to comply with the Act.

Decision notices

Anyone who has made a request for information under the Act can appeal or complain about the answer to that request. The first avenue of such action will be to the appropriate public authority's complaints procedure (see Chapter 2). If this fails to resolve a dispute, the complainant can apply to the Information Commissioner for a decision as to whether the public authority has made a correct decision under Part I of the Act.

If the complainant has not exhausted the relevant complaints procedure provided by the public authority or if the application:

- is frivolous or vexatious
- has been unduly delayed
- is withdrawn

the Information Commissioner must inform the complainant that a decision has not been reached and why.

If the Information Commissioner decides that a public authority has not complied with any of the provisions of Part I of the Act, such as:

- failing to communicate information
- failing to confirm or deny that information is held
- failing to comply with the applicant's preference for the way a request is answered
- failing to give the appropriate reasons for refusing a request or complying with the procedures for doing so

the Commissioner must issue a decision notice to both the complainant and the public authority. The notice must specify the steps which the public authority must take to comply with the requirement and the period within which they must be taken. It must also contain particulars of the right of appeal to the Information Tribunal.

If a decision notice is served on:

- a government department
- the National Assembly for Wales
- any public authority designated for these purposes by an Order made by the Lord Chancellor (under section 5 of the Act)

and the notice relates to the duty to confirm or deny or that the information is exempt information, that notice will have no effect, provided that within 20 working days of receipt of the notice by the public authority a certificate stating that the public authority has been correct in its response is given to the Information Commissioner. That certificate must be signed by the accountable person for the public authority. The 'accountable person' is:

- a Minister of the Crown who is a member of the Cabinet
- the Attorney-General, the Advocate-General for Scotland or the Attorney-General for Northern Ireland
- the First Minister and Deputy First Minister in Northern Ireland acting jointly, in relation to a Northern Ireland department or any Northern Ireland public authority
- the Assembly First Secretary, in relation to the National Assembly for Wales or any Welsh public authority.

Information notices

If the Information Commissioner has received a complaint on which the Commissioner needs to make a decision or has reason to believe that a public authority is not complying with the requirements of Part I of the Act or the Codes of Practice authorized by the Act, the Commissioner may require further information before issuing a decision notice, enforcement notice or practice recommendation. In these cases the Commissioner can serve an information notice on any public authority requiring it to provide specified information (including in this instance 'unrecorded information') to enable a conclusion to be reached regarding the decision or enforcement notices or practice recommendations. An information notice must contain:

- a statement that a complaint has been received
- a statement that the information required relates to the Information Commissioner's belief that the public authority is not complying with Part I of the Act or the Codes of Practice and
- reasons why the information would be relevant to that belief
- particulars of the right of appeal
- timescale for the response (bearing in mind the timescale for appeal).

The Act permits a public authority to refuse to supply information relating to any communication where legal professional privilege applies, where this may be in relation to advice or legal proceedings under the Act.

The Information Commissioner can cancel an information notice by written notice to the public authority concerned.

The power of the Information Commissioner to issue information notices in relation to publication schemes came into force on 30 November 2002.

Enforcement notices

If the Information Commissioner is satisfied that a public authority is not complying with a decision made by the Commissioner or is failing to make a decision itself under Part I of the Act, the Commissioner may serve the authority with an enforcement notice. An enforcement notice must contain:

- a statement of the provisions of Part I of the Act with which the public authority is not complying
- reasons why the Information Commissioner has reached the specified conclusions in this matter
- particulars of the right of appeal
- timescale for the response (bearing in mind the timescale for appeal).

The Information Commissioner may also suggest the steps which may be taken to comply with the Act's provisions.

If an enforcement notice is served on:

- a government department
- the National Assembly for Wales
- any public authority designated for these purposes by an Order made by the Lord Chancellor (under section 5 of the Act)

and the notice relates to the duty to confirm or deny or that the information is exempt information, that notice will have no effect, provided that within 20 working days of receipt of the notice by the public authority a certificate stating that the public authority has been correct in its response is given to the Information Commissioner. That certificate must be signed by the accountable person for the public authority. The 'accountable person' is:

- a Minister of the Crown who is a member of the Cabinet
- the Attorney-General, the Advocate-General for Scotland or the Attorney-General for Northern Ireland
- the First Minister and Deputy First Minister in Northern Ireland acting jointly, in relation to a Northern Ireland department or any Northern Ireland public authority
- the Assembly First Secretary, in relation to the National Assembly for Wales or any Welsh public authority.

The power of the Information Commissioner to issue enforcement notices in relation to publication schemes came into force on 30 November 2002.

Failure to comply with a notice

If a public authority fails to comply with either of the three notices, the Information Commissioner may write to the High Court or, in Scotland, the Court of Session certifying that the public authority has failed to comply with a notice. The court may deal with the public authority as if it had committed a contempt of court. Noncompliance includes any instance where an authority has knowingly or recklessly made a statement which it knows to be false when it purports to have complied with an information notice.

Appeals

A public authority or a complainant may appeal to the Information Tribunal against a decision notice, and a public authority may similarly appeal against an information notice or enforcement notice with which it has been served.

An appeal may be allowed on one of two grounds:

• the notice issued by the Information Commissioner is not in accordance with the law
• where the Information Commissioner used discretion and should have acted differently.

The Tribunal has the power to substitute another notice. Any party to an appeal to the Information Tribunal may appeal against the Tribunal's decision but only on a point of law. This would be made to the High Court of Justice in England (if the address of the public authority is in England or Wales), the Court of Session (if the address is in Scotland) or the High Court of Justice in Northern Ireland (if the address is in Northern Ireland).

These appeal procedures, with the exception of that against a decision notice, came into force on 30 November 2002.

Where a certificate has been issued by a Minister of the Crown to support either of the security exemptions in the Act, i.e.

• information supplied by, or relating to, bodies dealing with security matters
• national security

the Information Commissioner or any applicant whose request for information has been affected by the certificate may appeal to the Information Tribunal against the issue of the certificate. In the case of the national security exemption, the Tribunal is required to apply the same principles as those applied by a court on an applica-

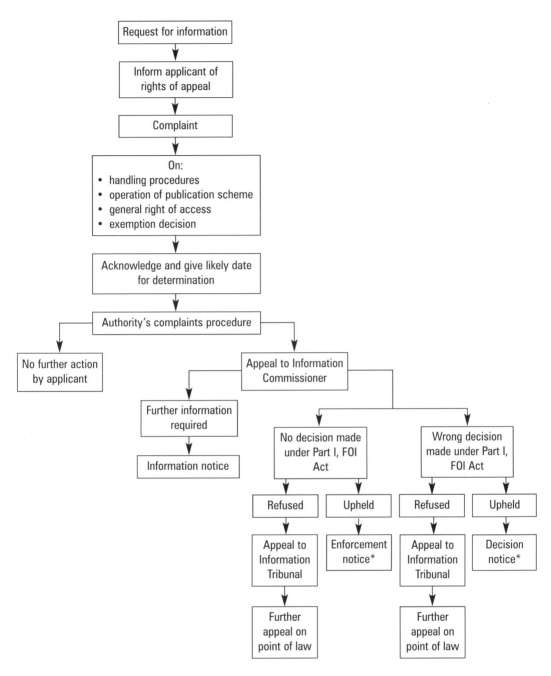

Figure 5.1   Summary of complaints and appeals procedures

tion for judicial review to judge whether a Minister had reasonable grounds for issuing a certificate. If during the appeal proceedings a public authority claims that it is possible to identify particular information from the general description given in the certificate, any other party to the proceedings may appeal to the Tribunal. In the absence of such an appeal, or if it is not successful, the certificate is deemed to apply.

As part of the duty to provide advice and assistance, public authorities would be well advised to prepare and publish a leaflet on the procedures for complaints and appeals. This might be a separate leaflet or part of general guidance on the handling of FOI requests. As a general rule documents should not be destroyed until the period for appeal has expired, even where they are included on a disposal schedule.

Figure 5.1 summarizes the complaints and appeals procedures described in this chapter.

6

Records management

Freedom of Information cannot be fully and effectively implemented without sound records management. The preface to the Lord Chancellor's Code of Practice on the Management of Records under section 46 of the Freedom of Information Act 2000 makes this important statement:

> **'Any freedom of information legislation is only as good as the quality of the records to which it provides access. Such rights are of little use if reliable records are not created in the first place, if they cannot be found when needed or if the arrangements for their eventual archiving or destruction are inadequate.'**

This chapter examines the issue of the need to maintain effective records so that the Act can be properly implemented. It describes the role of records in the effective discharge of an organization's functions and provides a detailed action plan for reaching compliance with the Code of Practice on the Management of Records under section 46 of the Act. It also provides practical guidance in undertaking an audit of records and information.

Records management and the Code of Practice

Records

Records are essential to the business of public authorities. They document the work of authorities, support their operations and form the basis for the many services that they provide. Records are essential to effective operations in several respects:

- Supporting the delivery of services – by documenting how policies and statutes are carried out, what services were provided, who carried out the work and how much it cost, and the authority's accomplishments.

- Supporting administration – by providing information for the direction, control, decision making and co-ordination of public authority work.
- Documenting rights and responsibilities – by providing evidence of the scope of a public authority's terms of reference, evidence of what it owns and evidence of its obligations. They are important also in documenting the rights of corporate bodies and individuals in matters such as ownership, legacy, etc.
- Legal documentation – many records comprise formal legal documents such as regulations, local orders, etc. – or formal documentation of the relationship between governments and people or institutions. They may, in this respect, be used in legal undertakings or be required for evidence in a court of law.
- Evidence of the work of public authorities – documentation of the decisions, actions and obligations of authorities, providing accountability measures.
- Future research – selected records of public authorities will form the contents of archival establishments and provide important historical information on political, social, economic and other issues.

Records are therefore created or received in the conduct of business activities and provide evidence and information about those activities. Records in all media are covered, including electronic records. A formal definition might be:

> Recorded information produced or received in the initiation, conduct or deletion of an institutional or individual activity, and which comprises sufficient content, context and structure to provide evidence of an activity, regardless of the form or medium.
>
> (International Council on Archives, 1997)

The management of records

Records management provides a framework which aims to ensure that:

- The record is present – the public authority has the information that is needed to ensure that it can reconstruct activities or transactions that have taken place.
- The record can be accessed – information can be located and used when required.
- The record can be interpreted – it is possible to establish its context – who created it, as part of which business process and how it relates to other records
- The record can be trusted – it reliably represents the information that was actually used in or created by the business process, and its integrity and authenticity can be demonstrated.
- The record can be maintained through time – the qualities of accessibility, interpretation and trustworthiness can be maintained for as long as the record is needed.
- The record will be disposed of as part of a planned system, through the implementation of disposal schedules to ensure the retention of the minimum volume of records consistent with effective and efficient operations.

The following principles underpin the management of records:

Records are a corporate resource

Records form part of the corporate memory of the authority and are a valuable corporate resource. From the point at which a document is created as a record, it becomes corporately owned.

Electronic records

Electronic records which are generated by or received in an authority in the course of its business are in this context no different from any other records – they are official, corporate records. Although most current practice is to print electronic information to paper, authorities should be making plans to maintain their electronic information as electronic records. Policies on modernizing government mean that, in order to preserve content and structure, records must be preserved as an electronic record. Records should be organized in a way that is able to meet anticipated future business and archival needs, and be reliably and consistently grouped regardless of media.

Record keeping should be integrated with business processes

Records management and archive administration must be built into systems for creating records, to ensure that they are capable of capturing records with all the necessary contextual information.

Records should be reliable, authentic and complete

Records should be able to function as evidence of business activities and processes through sound record-keeping practices. In order to be reliable and authentic they must adequately capture and describe the actions they represent and once created must not be altered without creating a new record. To be considered complete the record should preserve not only content but also the context in which it was created and used, and links to other records.

Records should be accessible

Record-keeping systems should aim to make records available quickly and easily to all staff and to others who are entitled to accessto , or information from, them.

Responsibility for capturing, maintaining and ensuring access to records rests with the organization as a whole

Responsibility for the capture and maintenance of records rests with everyone in the authority, and all staff should ensure that they are familiar with and are adhering to the records management policy and any procedures and guidelines that are issued through it.

Code of Practice

Authority for the Code of Practice on the Management of Records comes from section 46 of the Freedom of Information Act 2000:

> *The Lord Chancellor shall issue, and may from time to time revise, a code of practice providing guidance to relevant authorities as to the practice which it would, in his opinion, be desirable for them to follow in connection with the keeping, management and destruction of their records.*

The Code is a supplement to the provisions of the Freedom of Information Act 2000 and its adoption will help public authorities to comply with their duties under the Act.

Observance of the Code is promoted by the Information Commissioner in conjunction with the Keeper of Public Records. If it appears to the Commissioner that the practice of an authority in relation to the exercise of its functions under the FOI Act does not conform to that set out in the Code of Practice, the Commissioner may issue a practice recommendation under section 48 of the Act. Similarly, if the Commissioner reasonably requires information for the purpose of determining whether the practice of a public authority conforms with the Code of Practice, an information notice may be served under the provisions of section 51 of the FOI Act.

Failure to comply with the Code of Practice may mean that authorities are also failing to comply with other legislation, such as:

- Public Records Acts 1958 and 1967
- Public Records Act (NI) 1923
- Local Government (Records) Act 1962
- Local Government Act 1972
- Local Government (Access to Information) Act 1985
- Data Protection Act 1998
- Human Rights Act 1998

and thus may be in breach of their statutory obligations.

All communications in writing (including by electronic means) to a public authority fall within the scope of the Freedom of Information Act 2000, if they seek information, and must be dealt with in accordance with the provisions of the Act. It is therefore essential that everyone working in a public authority is familiar with the provisions of the Freedom of Information Act 2000, the Codes of Practice issued under its provisions, any relevant Memoranda of Understanding, and any relevant guidance on good practice issued by the Information Commissioner. Public authorities should therefore ensure that proper training is provided.

Developing records management compliant with the Code of Practice

Public authorities need to undertake nine major steps to reach compliance with the Code:

1 The records management function

Records management is a corporate function in a similar way to human resources, finance and estates management. The Code recommends that the function should be recognized as a specific corporate programme within a public authority and that it should receive the necessary levels of organizational support to ensure effectiveness. The function needs to bring together responsibilities for records in all formats from their creation to their ultimate disposal.

The person or persons responsible for the records management function should also have responsibility for, or close organizational connection with, the person or persons responsible for freedom of information, data protection and other information management issues. This will ensure co-ordinated and consistent progress towards the implementation of FOI and the achievement of other objectives under such directives as the *Modernising Government* agenda.

The person with responsibility for records management within a public authority should be someone of appropriate seniority that will enable them to promote and implement the requirements of the Code of Practice. The role should be formally acknowledged and made known throughout the authority. The responsibilities of a records manager would include overall supervision of the record-keeping arrangements in an authority and the provision of a source of advice and guidance on records to the authority generally. The job specification might include:

- Establish, develop and promote the strategy and programme for effective records management in the organization.
- Establish, develop and promote organization-wide standards for records management.
- Monitor the level of compliance with records management standards in all business areas, and identify and encourage any action required.

- Operational responsibilities:
  - — Provide written and verbal advice and consultancy to staff at all levels on all aspects of information management.
  - — Maintain knowledge of new developments in legislation surrounding information management, and records management systems and technologies.
  - — Develop and maintain links with operational business areas of the organization.
  - — Identify and manage records management projects, identify resources, timescales and budgets as required.
- Skills and knowledge:
  - — strong analytical skills, with the ability to absorb and manipulate new information quickly
  - — excellent written and oral communication skills; the ability to listen, influence, guide and persuade staff at all levels
  - — initiative in developing solutions to new problems; ability to act independently and think outside the framework of current procedures, and challenge assumptions, producing creative solutions to problems
  - — good planning and time management skills
  - — computer literacy
  - — knowledge of the 'particular part of the public sector' environment
  - — maintain standards; promoting quality improvement throughout the organization and providing management information as required.

2 Roles and responsibilities of records managers

Records management responsibilities should be clearly defined and assigned in a public authority, and made known throughout the organization. Records managers, their staff and all who are concerned with the management of information need to develop particular knowledge and skills in order to comply with records management requirements, to ensure the effective operation of the authority and its business, to provide the means for achieving corporate objectives, and to contribute to the Government's overall policy of modernizing the public service. Responsibilities for undertaking records management roles should be set out in a performance agreement, role description or similar document.

Roles and responsibilities can be set within a framework of competency standards and job specifications drawn up from it. These standards should describe what people do in the workplace; identify the characteristics, knowledge and skills possessed or required by individuals that will enable them to undertake their duties effectively; and cover all aspects of records management performance (skills and knowledge, attitudes, communication, application and development). Such a framework is described in detail in Chapter 8. While the size and available resources of some organizations may mean that all the roles and responsibilities described are not present or possible, the framework is flexible enough to be adapted to suit particular needs. At the end of the day public authorities must have the knowledge and expertise to enable them to manage their records and information in such a way that they are able to meet all their statutory obligations, particularly those of the Freedom of Information Act 2000.

3 Records management policy statement

A policy statement on how the authority manages its records should be drawn up and made available to all staff. This will provide an authoritative statement on the management of records and ensure that business information is managed effectively throughout the authority. The aim of the statement should be to provide a record-keeping system which will:

- meet the authority's business needs
- address the needs of the authority's stakeholders
- conform to relevant legislation, regulations and standards
- provide a basis for accountability
- identify responsibilities for records and information, in particular the role of the records manager.

The statement should provide the framework for supporting standards and guidance, and cover all aspects of records management, in particular:

- an authority's commitment to create, keep and manage records which document its principal activities
- the role of records management and its relationship to the authority's overall strategy
- the responsibility of individuals to document their actions and decisions
- the disposal of records and information
- an indication of the way in which compliance with the policy and its supporting standards and guidance will be monitored.

4 Training and awareness

Training in records management takes place at two levels – professional development for records management staff and awareness of records issues by all members of staff.

Induction programmes should include awareness sessions on record keeping and might cover the following brief points:

- the role of records management in the authority
- responsibilities of individuals
- the value of good record keeping
- provision of standards, guidance and advice.

A programme of professional training of records management staff should be available on a regular basis. The programme should identify particular training needs in the light of the competency framework, of new legislation and of developments in technology, and arrange for those needs to be met, using internal or external training as appropriate. Ideas for particular training are described in Chapter 8.

5 Records creation

Authorities should have in place a record-keeping system that documents its activities and provides for the quick and easy retrieval of information.

Records are created and included in a classification system to provide formal evidence of the business transactions of the authority. The purpose of files and folders is to capture, maintain and provide access to evidence of transactions over time in accordance with accountability and business practices. The establishment of a coherent classification system provides for faster and systematic filing, faster retrieval of information, greater protection of information, and increased administrative stability, continuity and efficiency.

The system should include:

- classification of the records into series that have meaningful titles and a consistent reference code
- responsibility on individuals creating records to allocate them to a series and, if necessary, a sub-series
- sequences of reference numbers that can cover series with both electronic and paper records
- checking/monitoring scheme
- audit of the references used so that the classification system makes sense and records can be found in appropriate search sequences.

Information about records should also be maintained, including the contents of files and folders, how they are organized, and who created and used them. This information will be generally available at the time the records are created and it should be recorded for use at future stages in the records life cycle. The items of information listed in Table 6.1 should be recorded. Table 6.1 includes reference to the cross-government metadata standard.

The records classification system should include a set of rules or a manual which will enable it to be easily understood and promote the efficient retrieval of information.

Table 6.1 Information about records

Item	Description	Cross-government
Series identifier	Usually the title and an alphabetical or alpha numeric prefix (e.g. 2/FIN/)	Aggregation level
Format and structure	Physical nature of the series or collection and a description of the filing system	Format
Index or finding aid	Method by which access to the series or collection is given (e.g. computer database or simple card index)	Location
Time span	Start and end dates of the series, and of individual records	Date: open date and close date
Subject matter	Purpose for which the records were collected or created, such as reference to any relevant legislation	Subject keywords
Creators	Department, division or unit which created the records	Creator
Users	Departments, divisions or units which had access to the records and used them in the course of their work	
Related records	Include earlier and later series	Relation
Disposal	Appraisal criteria applied, including references to any operational selection policy, and any disposal schedule applying to the series or collection	Disposal
Access	Any restrictions on the information contained in the series, either under legislative provisions or sensitivity criteria	Rights
Transferred records	Information about records transferred, migrated or separated from the series and about any records which have been re-registered in the series	

6 Record maintenance

The record-keeping system should be maintained so that the records and information are properly stored and protected, and so that they can be easily located and retrieved.

A system to track the movement and location of records should be used so that information can be retrieved at any time and so that there is an auditable trail of record transactions. This system might take the form of location cards (which take the place of a file on a shelf), docket books, diary cards, bar-coding, transfer slips, or an electronic records management system. Tracking should record the following information:

- item reference number or identifier
- description of the item
- person, position or operational area having possession or use of the item
- date of movement.

Maintenance procedures should include a contingency or business recovery plan. This should provide for protection of those records and information which are vital to the continuing operation of the authority, and plans on recovery should a disaster occur.

7 Record disposal

Public authorities should have in place clearly defined arrangements for the appraisal and selection of records, and for documenting such work. Records and information should be kept for as long as they are needed to meet the operational needs of the authority, and to meet legal and regulatory requirements. They need to be assessed to determine:

- their value as a source of information about the authority, its operations, relationships and environment
- their importance as evidence of business activities and decisions
- whether there are any legal or regulatory retention requirements
- any historical value.

The following retention periods might typically be allocated when appraising paper records:

- 2 years – information which is required for reference and for which this need will have evaporated after two years; records in this category are generally distinguished by the description 'used once, unlikely to be required again'.
- 5 years – information which is likely to be required to inform current practice and procedure; business processes and planning will usually have moved on after five years.
- Variable – 1) legal retention (for example, certain financial records); 2) generic information (for example, personnel records) in line with central guidance
- 25 years – records which are likely to have historical value.

The timeframe in which action to appraise and preserve access to electronic records can be taken is shorter than with conventional records due to:

- the pace of technological change in the systems which create, store and access records
- the instability of the media on which records are held
- the danger of technological obsolescence.

Electronic records should be appraised at an early stage to avoid the risk of the information becoming incomplete or unreliable, or changes in information technology systems causing the loss or degradation of records which may not have been transferred to a new system with sufficient forethought. The appraisal should be carried out, at the most, within five years of creation of the earliest records within a system; ideally, it should be undertaken at the time of system design and installation.

Disposal schedules

Disposal schedules are key documents in the management of records and information. A schedule is simply a list of series or collections of records for which predetermined periods of retention have been agreed between the operational manager and the records manager.

Records on disposal schedules will fall into three main categories:

- Destroy after an agreed period – where the useful life of a series or collection of records can be easily predetermined (for example, destroy after three years; destroy two years after the end of the financial year).
- Automatically select for permanent preservation – where certain groups of records can be readily defined as worthy of permanent preservation and transferred to an appropriate archive.
- Appraise – see above.

Disposal policies should be examined every three years to ensure that new developments or regulations are taken fully into account and that retention periods are still realistic in the light of any changes in the business of the authority.

8 Access

Public authorities should have in place clearly defined arrangements for documenting FOI exemption and closure decisions. These decisions are subject to appeal under Part V of the Freedom of Information Act 2000 and their documentation may be required in that connection. It is recommended that records relating to FOI requests be kept as follows:

- 1 year – for documents already open
- 2 years – for documents which are subsequently opened
- 10 years – for documents which remain closed.

9 Performance measurement

The records management system should be monitored regularly to ensure that information is being managed effectively and that policies and procedures comply with the requirements of business and legislation. Authorities should use a set of performance indicators to help them in this respect; these will also be valuable in undertaking resource planning and organizing workflow arrangements. They might include the following:

- quantity of records created (in linear metres or megabytes)
- response times in providing information from the records or retrieving the records themselves
- quantity of records appraised, selected and destroyed or transferred to an archive
- user satisfaction.

Model action plan for records management

The report of the Advisory Group on Openness in the Public Sector (December 1999) recommended that all public authorities should develop records management action plans detailing the steps which they will take to reach the standards set out in the Code of Practice under section 46 of the FOI Act. To assist in this process the National Archives undertook to produce model action plans for public authorities to use as the basis for their own action plans.

Different parts of the public sector have different requirements in this area. Although the main elements of a model action plan would be relevant to all, some minor issues might not be. Accordingly variations to the model plan are available, aimed at different parts of the public sector:

- central government
- local government
- further education and higher education organizations
- police authorities
- the National Health Service
- schools.

These can be found on the National Archives website: www.nationalarchives/gov/uk.

The model plan focuses on the actions required to prepare records management practices specifically for the FOI Act. Many of the actions are similar to those required in preparing for electronic records management. The plans do not suggest that the two sets of actions need to be carried out separately for the different purposes, but rather provide a checklist of FOI requirements so that they can be built into existing activities wherever possible. In many cases existing activities may need only to be extended slightly.

The action plans focus on how information is acquired, and how it should be organized and retrieved, so that responses to FOI requests can be dealt with quickly and efficiently. While the timing of each action point is indicative, it is important to follow the sequence of steps in any plan.

Table 6.2 summarizes the action points and provides a recommended timetable.

Table 6.2 Timetable of action points in model plan

Completion by	Milestone	Code of Practice Reference	Related Electronic Records Management milestones*
31 July 2003	1. Undertake an audit of records management to establish the need for action to reach compliance with the Code		
	2. Examine functional organization to see whether responsibility for FOI implementation and departmental records can be placed in the same area	5.1	
	3. Analyse business activities in preparation for drafting a records management policy statement	6	
	4. Establish a competency framework to identify skills and knowledge required by records management staff	7.3	
	5. Establish the need, or otherwise, for records management support staff	7.3	
	6. Make available the agreed records management policy statement	6	Corporate Policy on Electronic Records (October 2000)
30 September 2003	1. Recruit records management support staff, if required	7.3	
	2. Draw up a programme on awareness of records management issues for inclusion in induction training	7.3	
1 January 2004	1. Ensure that all information functions are part of the same command or that there are close working relationships between them	5.1	Strategy for ERM in e-business plans (October 2000); and Strategic Plan for corporate ERM (September 2001)
	2. Introduce a programme of professional training for records management staff	7.3	
	3. Complete an information survey	8.4	Inventory of existing electronic records (December 2000)
	4. Design and implement a system to ensure that records are appraised in good time	9.4	Appraisal and preservation plans (September 2001)
	5. Design and implement a system for documenting appraisal decisions	9.5	
	6. Design and implement a system for documenting disclosure and non-disclosure decisions	8	
	7. Have in place a system for preparing schedules about access to records being transferred to a record office	11.7 and 11.8	
1 June 2004	1. Ensure that adequate resources are in place to support the records management function	7.3	

Continued on next page

Table 6.2 *Continued*

Completion by	Milestone	Code of Practice Reference	Related Electronic Records Management milestones*
	2. Ensure that record-keeping systems are in place to meet operational needs and accord with the regulatory environment	8.5 and 8.6	Detailed requirements for corporate ERM (March 2002)
	3. Ensure that records maintenance procedures are in place to enable the quick and efficient location and retrieval of information	8.7 and 8.8	
	4. Ensure that a business recovery plan is in place	8.9	
1 January 2005	Establish a performance measurement scheme for the records management system	6.2	

* These relate to the *Modernising Government* agenda (central government requirements, as laid out in the White Paper *Modernising Government* (Cm. 4130, 1999)).

Records audit

A records audit is essential for an authority to know what information it holds and thus to respond to requests for information in accordance with the FOI Act. It is also a prerequisite for the work of the records manager. Records are the reflection of an organization's activities. The audit provides access to these activities and the records that arise from them. It profiles each record series and system, and helps to identify any problems, establish a records management programme, and quickly to design a filing system or produce a disposal schedule. It also helps to determine what is required to install and maintain the records management programme (space, equipment, personnel, etc.) as well as how to evaluate the efficacy and economy of records management systems, particularly in the context of the preparation for FOI implementation.

An audit gives an objective view of an organization's record collections and their uses. It is the first and most important step to the proper control of records whereby procedures are considered in a systematic and disciplined way. It is also a useful tool in assessing the level of knowledge of records management in an organization.

The collection and analysis of data from an information survey is time-consuming and labour intensive. Comprehensiveness and the productive use to which the information gathered can be put need to be balanced.

Records audits are primarily concerned with the examination of active records but occasionally it may be necessary to survey semi-active or inactive material when, for example, retention periods are being re-examined.

Content

In order to meet records management objectives and users' needs, having regard to the likely availability of resources, the records audit needs to include the following:

- a full understanding of the organization – the nature of its activities, its mission, objectives, components and operations
- level of staff awareness of records management
- what records are held and the activities to which they relate
- an inventory of record containers (cabinets, shelves, etc.)
- records documentation (file lists, indexes, etc.)
- amount of records
- copies of records
- date range of records
- frequency of consultation of the records
- tracking systems for the records
- current records management system and competence levels of records management staff.

Methodology for a records audit

Planning

Many of the difficulties associated with introducing new records management procedures can be overcome by careful planning of the audit. This planning should include:

- commitment from top management
- aims and objectives
- communication
- data collection.

Commitment from top management

Written authority from top management for the audit to be conducted and advanced warning to staff of the organization will go a long way towards producing an effective records audit. A programme of visits to offices should be agreed and the objectives of the audit communicated to the staff involved.

Aims and objectives

Aims and objectives must be established before the audit is undertaken. These parallel the objectives of records management in general and are actually part of the strategy in achieving these objectives. They may be short-term or long-term.

Short-term objectives are usually the basics of records management improvement programmes:

- development of economical records storage and retrieval
- improvement of active records management systems
- development of disposal schedules.

Other objectives may be of less immediate concern, such as forms control or computerization.

The objective of the audit should therefore be to gather only the information that addresses the aims and objectives cited above. For example:

- Identification of all the organization's records by series or collection and an understanding of their functional context will provide the basis for the disposal schedule.
- Categorization of the types of equipment will assist in systems improvement and in calculating savings.

Communication

Prior to carrying out the audit a notice should be sent to all managers and staff concerned, identifying the nature of the audit, its objectives, how it will affect their work, and when it will begin. It is often useful to hold orientation sessions with key staff, and to keep managers informed by the issue of progress reports.

Data collection

Before conducting the audit several items should be collected and studied:

- costs of office space, equipment, supplies and staff; organizational unit costs are often calculated regularly for accommodation (including maintenance and running costs) and for staff (including support services)
- maps and plans of buildings, showing furniture and equipment
- copies of contracts with commercial storage companies, microfilming bureaux, computer services, etc.
- inventory of equipment, including computers and photocopiers
- organization charts that give an understanding of the flow of information
- procedural manuals and forms
- copies of file lists or databases
- copies of previous studies.

There are two main alternative methods of collecting data in a records audit: physical observation or questionnaire.

Physical observation

A physical survey requires records staff to visit operational areas and look into each item of records storage equipment, ask questions and complete a standard form. Individual records need not be examined; it is usually sufficient to sample a series or collection.

The physical survey should be carefully planned and executed with a minimum of disruption. An initial investigation to establish the whereabouts, ownership, volume and condition of the records may be required to make the plan more effective. When the plan and timetable have been drawn up the detailed survey can follow, using standard forms that are simple and straightforward.

Four main actions form the key to finding out information from the survey:

- find every storage place with records and information, including tops of cabinets, disks, commercial storage, under desks
- look at all the records and information in the location and media discovered
- ask questions until understanding is complete
- record the information acquired for future analysis.

Questionnaire

The reliability of data which might be required to develop or support a hypothesis or serve as a prerequisite for introducing new procedures is closely related to the size of the survey through which the data are obtained. Physical surveys can be programmed to cover all parts of an organization. The use of questionnaires, however, relies on individuals to complete them accurately and in good time. Because of the heterogeneous nature of information resources, careful consideration should be given before deciding whether the use of a questionnaire will provide results comprehensive enough to enable crucial decisions to be made. Although a well constructed questionnaire which produces a high-percentage response can be a sound, cost-effective approach to gathering information, greater coverage is likely to be achieved through physical observation.

Questions must be framed so that they elicit relevant and accurate information. They can be open or closed. Open questions will encourage opinions and give freedom to respondents but the analysis of free-ranging responses can be difficult. Closed questions lessen the chance of obtaining information which might be useful but which may not have been thought of. A balance of closed and open questions is ideal.

Open questions should direct the respondent to as specific an area as possible. For example, the following questions will produce different responses:

A. Having recently attended a records management course, what are your thoughts?
B. You recently attended a records management course. What new skills do you think you acquired?

Closed questions can be asked in a variety of ways:

• seeking a yes or no answer
• providing statement or answer boxes for ticks
• ranking scales, for levels of agreement to statements or order of priority of certain issues.

Whatever method or type of questioning is used, only one answer should be sought to one question. For example, the following is actually asking two questions:

> There have been too many leaks of confidential papers and managers should be doing more to prevent leaks occurring.
>
> Agree………..l………..l………..l………..l………..Disagree

Consideration should be given to the issue of anonymity. If names are not included on completed questionnaires it may cause difficulties in checking the extent of replies received.

Data required from a records audit are largely factual rather than consisting of opinions. Interpretation of the data is therefore not problematic with questionnaires, although the lack of comprehensiveness (if not all questionnaires are returned) may invalidate some of the data. The degree of invalidation may make it necessary to undertake some physical observation.

However, a good way of collecting the necessary information for an audit can be a combination of physical observation and questionnaire. The questionnaire can be sent to the person most likely to have the knowledge and expertise about record keeping in each of the operational areas of the organization. They should be asked to complete the form as far as possible but be told that it is not necessary to return it; it is being given mainly to highlight those issues that need to be addressed as part of the audit. At an appropriate time an informal interview can be held with the person when both parties can work through the questionnaire and confirm or clarify the information required.

Specimen questionnaire

[*The Organization*]

Questionnaire on the Management of Records and Information

I should be most grateful if you could take some time out to complete the attached questionnaire prior to our meeting on xxxxxxxxxx. It should help to save time at the meeting and give us a good pointer to the type of information held and how it is used and disposed of.

Continued on next page

If you would like to include any extra information or need to use an extra sheet, please attach the papers to the form. You need not return the form – it is being used to guide you in the direction of the records issues that will be raised.

Glossary of terms used:

Section	a section/unit within a division working on a specific area of work; where the division has a single function the term section should be interpreted as the division
Disposal	the review and subsequent retention or destruction of records
Information	covering records in all formats (paper, electronic, etc.)
Registered file	official file forming part of a discrete series, classified and referenced in accordance with accepted practice
Review	examination of a record to see if it has any further administrative or historical use
Unregistered file	informal folders or information held by individuals, neither of which are on a standard system
Vital records	those records without which a section could not continue to operate, and which contain information needed to re-establish the section in the event of a disaster

Thank you for your help

---

1. Date completed: 2. Branch and function:

---

3. Person completing form and contact details:

---

4. What main categories of information does your section hold? (e.g. planning applications, registers of electors, policy files)

Continued on next page

5. How is information held in
   your section? Please tick formats
   below (take all categories as
   one source of information):

6. How much of this information
   is held on more than one of the
   formats (%)?

– registered files
– unregistered
– floppy disk
– network drive
– personal network drive
– personal disk drive
– other

7. Does your section have a policy for disposal of your records, including
   electronic?

If so, please give outline details (continue on a separate sheet):

8. What do you consider to be
   your vital records?

9. What indexes/finding aids does the
   section hold to help you locate
   records? (e.g. manual list, database)
   Do you use standard terms/naming
   conventions?

10. How much of the information held by your section is not used for current
    work (%) (including off-site storage)?

11. Where and how does your section store records? (e.g. 4-drawer cabinets,
    open shelves, etc.) Please indicate how many items of each type of
    equipment.

Continued on next page

12. What and how much (%)
    information is currently made
    available to:
    the general public?

13. Please indicate what and how much
    other information in your section, if
    any, could be made available to:
    the general public?

shared with other branches in [x]?

shared with other branches in [x]?

other authorities/organizations?

other authorities/organizations?

14. What requests do you receive for the information that your section holds?
    (please tick)

    Public representatives (MPs, etc.)   *Internal*

    Companies/organizations   *Public*

15. How much time do you spend looking for information each week?
    (please tick)

    Less than 1 hr   1–3 hrs   4–6 hrs   7–10 hrs   Over 10 hrs

16. How often do you NOT find what you want? (please tick)

    Never   Rarely   Sometimes   Often   Constantly

Costs

An analysis of the costs of the records operations should be an integral part of the records audit. Background information will need to be obtained from a central source and used in conjunction with the results of the audit as part of the overall evaluation and report.

Accommodation costs vary from building to building and location to location. For example, office accommodation (such as active records management units or registries) is usually considerably more expensive than storage accommodation (file stores, intermediate repositories, records centres, etc.) simply because of the nature of the services required by each (telecommunications, electricity, lighting, messengerial, etc.).

Staff costs are generally standardized for particular levels of work throughout public services. Information should be available from departmental financial services.

Equipment costs are crucial to an evaluation of a survey's results. Some types of equipment are more cost-effective than others (for example, lateral filing cupboards compared to four-drawer filing cabinets) and a careful analysis of their relative costs, including any maintenance, is important for reaching cost-effective solutions or improvements in records management procedures.

Comparison of storage costs is most easily achieved by calculating a storage factor for each type of equipment. This is simply the result of dividing the amount of files (in linear metres) by the area occupied (in square metres), including the area necessary to access the records. The higher the storage factor the more efficient is the equipment.

Calculating the storage factor

- A four-drawer filing cabinet holds 2.5 m of records and occupies 2.25 sq m of space; the storage factor is therefore 1.11.
- A lateral filing cupboard holds 4 m of records and occupies 0.77 sq m of space; the storage factor is therefore 5.2.

The accommodation, staff and equipment costs should be aggregated on a monthly and yearly basis. Projections and evaluations can then be made, using different storage equipment, accommodation or staff.

Estimates for different storage equipment

File Series: 2/GEN   Year: 1999/00

Amount of files: 80 metres

Location: Britannia House, Brighton

Continued on next page

Equipment:	4-drawer filing cabinets	Lateral filing cupboards
Space occupied:	75 sq metres	15.4 sq metres
Accommodation cost @ £200 / sq m / pa:	£15,000 pa	£3,080 pa
Saving:	–	£11,920 pa

Evaluation

The task of analysis and evaluation of the data from the audit should be carried out promptly as delay can make the findings obsolete. Evaluation should be made with a use for the information in mind. Records management is meant to improve records and information systems for the people who use them. An audit that results in only a statistical report is of no use. Information gathered from the audit should enable consideration of the following:

- records which are valueless and could be destroyed immediately – identified from the survey form by low or nil usage rate, or duplication
- inactive records which could be removed to storage – closed files no longer required for reference which can be removed to cheaper accommodation
- filing equipment which could be emptied, removed or reused – the survey may identify partially filled equipment in which records could be consolidated
- computers being used inefficiently – the evaluation should take the opportunity to assess whether computerized filing systems, indexes or databases are being put to good use and are improving the efficiency of the information systems
- records or information which could be consolidated, including the elimination or reduction of duplication – evidence of duplication should be highlighted so that resources are used most efficiently
- protection of the records against loss, damage, etc. – the type of equipment used should take into account the value of the records, including those which may be of archival value
- effectiveness of systems (filing, indexing, etc.) – staff and user comments may point the way to the need for improvement.

Only when issues such as these have been considered can plans for improvement, appraisal or new programmes begin.

Presentation of results

Quantitative data from the audit can be presented in tabular form (e.g. number of different types of storage equipment), with charts (e.g. percentage of records covered by disposal schedules) or by graphs (e.g. comparison of number of staff and amount of records serviced). Qualitative data, such as physical condition or staff comments, will need to be presented in narrative form.

The audit report should frame recommendations that are clear and constructive proposals for improvement or development. They should be short and supported by facts in the report. They may be:

- Educational – Where the recommendation is long-term or developmental, a timetable should be considered.
- Influential – Where contact or negotiation and persuasion are needed, consideration should be given to who the important figures might be, whether they have been involved, and who might be able to contribute to implementation of the recommendation.
- Challenging – Where some areas might be directly challenged by a recommendation, the balancing advantages must be taken into account.
- Enforcing – Tightening up of procedures may lead to significant changes in culture or attitude.
- Redeploying – Where existing procedures or systems may have to change, there may also be implications in budgets, timetable, training, etc.
- Cost saving – Where costs can be measured with reasonable certainty, the report should set out the cost benefits clearly.

The audit report should be as short as possible. There should be a summary concentrating on major findings and recommendations, a brief narrative to illustrate evidence gathered during the survey, and factual data.

Advice and guidance

The National Archives have produced several series of standards and guidance on the management of records and information. Although these are aimed primarily at central government departments and agencies, they can be freely adapted to the needs of other bodies in the public sector. Access to these series is through the National Archives website: www.pro.gov.uk/recordsmanagement/standardsandguidance.

The Records Management Society has been instrumental in developing retention scheduling guidance for local authorities, as well as several other valuable pieces of advice. See its website: www.rms-gb.org.uk.

In the further education sector the Joint Information Services Committee has produced much valuable advice and guidance, especially on the management of electronic information. Its website is: www.jisc.ac.uk.

The Association of Chief Police Officers (ACPO) set up an FOI project in 2001 and has more recently produced some records management guidance, most notably on retention scheduling. Contact with ACPO can be made through its website: www.acpo.police.uk.

In the health sector the Controls Assurance Support Unit (CASU) has produced a records management standard and the Department of Health has issued a circular on the management of records in the NHS (HC 053/99, *For the Record*) which includes a model schedule for NHS records. There is also a valuable guide on the retention and disposal of patients' records published by the Health Archives Group, which is available on the National Archives website. See: www.casu.org.uk and www.doh.gov.uk/.

7

Data protection, human rights and other legislation

This chapter describes the relationships between the FOI Act and other legislation, most notably that relating to data protection, human rights and environmental information. Staff in public authorities may specialize in particular areas of information policy and legislation (such as data protection, freedom of information or environmental information) but there needs to be an integrated information maintenance and access regime. Synergy of the various regulations and codes of practice is vital if an organization is to discharge its responsibilities effectively.

Data protection

The two main areas in which the Freedom of Information Act 2000 affects data protection are:

- the enforcement of both data protection and freedom of information by one person (the Information Commissioner)
- the definition of personal data.

Enforcement

With the passing of the Act the Data Protection Commissioner became the Information Commissioner, now responsible for supervising the implementation of both the data protection and the freedom of information legislation. At first sight this appears to be a conflict of interest, and there is no doubt that there is a certain tension between the two Acts. However, the Freedom of Information Act counters this quite effectively by making most applications for personal data exempt under section 40. When the freedom of information legislation was being drafted and debated, many argued that, if any conflict between privacy and openness were to arise, then let it be resolved by one person.

Definition of personal data

The Data Protection Act 1998 (DP Act) defines 'data' as:

information which –

(a) *is being processed by means of equipment operating automatically in response to instructions given for that purpose,*
(b) *is recorded with the intention that it should be processed by means of such equipment,*
(c) *is recorded as part of a relevant filing system or with the intention that it should form part of a relevant filing system, or*
(d) *does not fall within paragraph (a), (b) or (c) but forms part of an accessible record as defined by section 68 . . .*[1]

It defines 'personal data' as:

data which relate to a living individual who can be identified –

(a) *from those data, or*
(b) *from those data and other information which is in the possession of, or is likely to come into the possession of, the data controller,*

and includes any expressions of opinion about the individual and any indication of the intentions of the data controller or any other person in respect of the individual.

A relevant filing system is regarded under the Data Protection Act as any set of information relating to individuals that is structured by reference to individuals or by reference to criteria relating to individuals, in such a way that information relating to a particular individual is readily accessible. It includes information processed automatically (i.e. by computer) and manually (i.e. paper and other systems).

The Freedom of Information Act 2000 extends the definition of personal data to include all information – not just that in a relevant filing system – in relation to organizations which are public authorities under the Act. This may have significant implications for managers in particular. Where they have kept loose information on their staff to help them in, for example, annual assessments, such information may now be accessed by the individuals. However, not all the data subject's rights are applicable to this extended category of data. They can see the data and request any inaccuracies to be amended, but they cannot prevent use of the data for the purposes of direct marketing and retention of the data for longer than is necessary for a specific purpose. In addition there are some procedural requirements for accessing unstructured data.

In essence the right of access to information about third parties under the Freedom of Information Act is subject to three main conditions:

- Disclosure should not contravene the eight Data Protection Principles, i.e.
  1 Fair and lawful processing
  2 Processing for a specified and lawful purpose
  3 Data not to be excessive
  4 Accuracy of the data
  5 Data not to be kept longer than necessary
  6 Data subject rights
  7 Security
  8 Transfer outside the EU.
- Information would be disclosed to the data subject (of the information) if they applied under the Data Protection Act 1998 provisions.
- The data subject(s) have not exercised their right to prevent processing likely to cause damage or distress.

While private personal data (home address, marital status, personal life, etc.) would not be disclosed under the new arrangements, it is likely that some information about public servants in connection with their work will be accessible, for example work telephone number and address, role, responsibilities and grade.

The use and making available of personal data under the Data Protection Act 1998 is a very complex area, and strictly not within the scope of this work. For freedom of information purposes the main point is that requests for personal information by the subject of that data must be dealt with under the data protection legislation. Similar requests from a third party must be dealt with under the freedom of information legislation. Figure 7.1 will help public authorities to deal with requests for personal information.

Human rights

All public authorities, including those which for one reason or another are not subject to the Freedom of Information Act 2000 and those bodies which have a mixture of private and public functions, are public authorities under the Human Rights Act 1998. This Act makes it unlawful for any public authority to act in a way that is incompatible with the European Convention on Human Rights.

There are five articles of the Convention which have a bearing on freedom of information:

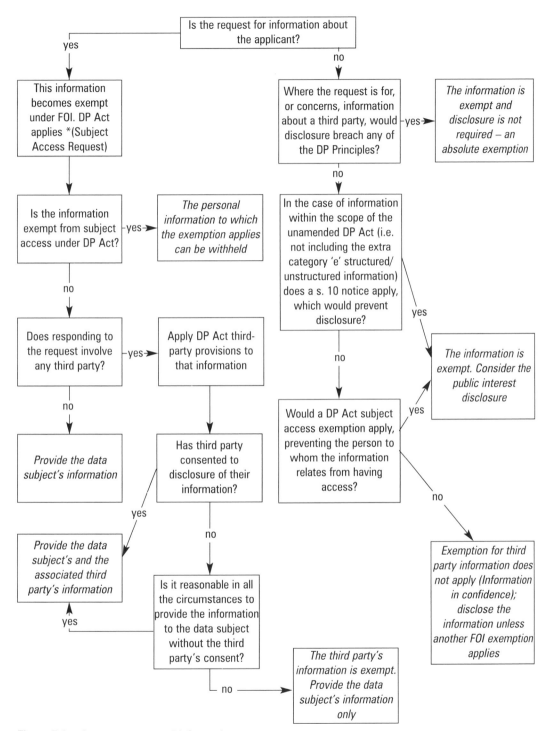

Figure 7.1 Access to personal information

*Request by an individual for information about themselves.

- Article 2: Right to life – The provision of information relating to health and safety may affect this protection of the right to life.
- Article 5: Right to liberty and security – The right to access to information may be necessary in providing an individual with the right of access to a court to test the lawfulness of detention under this article.
- Article 6: Right to a fair trial – Defendants in criminal cases may be able to argue that it is in the public interest for information on the investigation to be disclosed.
- Article 8: Respect for private and family life – As well as private and family life, this includes the individual's home and correspondence. Thus there may be a request for access to information that contravenes this article.
- Article 10: Freedom of expression – The right also includes freedom to receive and impart information.

Like the Data Protection Act 1998, there seems to be a tension between freedom of information and human rights, and the relationship is no less complicated. Where the European Convention on Human Rights allows the release of information, it will be unlawful for a public authority to withhold that information. The Information Commissioner will be able to interpret the Act in such a way that the public interest test can be applied in such circumstances.

Environmental Information Regulations

Prior to the Environmental Information Regulations 1992, the Environmental Protection Act 1990 granted public access to various pollution registers.

A right of access to information relating to the environment held by public authorities has been provided by the Environmental Information Regulations 1992 and by the Environmental Information (Amendment) Regulations 1998. These regulations require public authorities to make available information about the condition of the environment, anything which has a negative effect upon it, and what measures are being taken to counter the negative effects. From a practical point of view these Regulations:

- apply to a wider range of public authorities than the Freedom of Information Act
- apply to all requests for environmental information (not just written requests)
- have fewer potential grounds for refusal
- override domestic information regimes.

The Aarhus Convention of 1998 is intended to increase public access to environmental information by:

- clarifying the definition of 'environmental information'
- introducing a public interest test to apply to all exceptions with a tighter constraint on the refusal of information on emissions

- shortening time lines for responses to requests for information from 'as soon as possible' and 'within two months' to one month, which can be extended to two months where necessary
- introducing provisions relating to the format of information, the provision of advice and assistance, and the transfer of requests
- requiring the proactive dissemination of information.

A new European Directive (2003/4/EC) has introduced further changes. These include:

- clarification of the term 'public authority'
- amending requirements on the handling of information on emissions
- tightening requirements on charging for environmental information to allow public authorities to charge for the cost of supplying information only
- introducing personal data provisions to align the environmental requirements with data protection.

The Freedom of Information Act provides that the Secretary of State may make regulations to implement the Aarhus Convention. New regulations are expected in 2004. These will harmonize the environmental information and freedom of information regimes (for example, 20 working days' deadline, criminal sanctions).

It was agreed in 1999 that the Environmental Information Regulations should be exempt from the FOI Act to avoid the risk of not meeting international obligations and to allow for updating the regulations. It was also agreed that environmental information should be treated no differently from any other information and that the provisions of the FOI Act relating to the Information Commissioner and the Information Tribunal would also apply to the Environmental Information Regulations.

Under the Environmental Information Regulations information relates to the environment if it relates to any of the following:

- the state of any water or air, the state of any flora or fauna, the state of any soil or the state of any natural site or other land
- any activities or measures (including activities giving rise to noise or any other nuisance) which adversely affect anything mentioned above or are likely to affect anything so mentioned
- any activities or administrative or other measures (including any environmental management programmes) which are designed to protect anything mentioned above.

The 1998 Regulations amend the 1992 section on confidential information to:

- affect international relations, national defence or public security

- affect matters which are, or have been, an issue in any legal proceedings or in any enquiry, or are the subject matter of any investigation undertaken with a view to any such proceedings or enquiry
- affect the confidentiality of the deliberations of any relevant person
- involve the supply of a document or other record which is still in course of completion, or of any internal communication of a relevant person
- affect the confidentiality of matters to which any commercial or industrial confidentiality attaches, including intellectual property.

Information must be treated as confidential if:

- it is capable of being so treated and its disclosure in response to a request would contravene any statutory provision or rule of law or would involve a breach of any agreement [2]
- the information is personal information contained in records held in relation to an individual who has not given their consent to its disclosure
- the information is held by the relevant person in consequence of having been supplied by a person who:
    — was not under, and could not have been put under, any legal obligation to supply it to the relevant person
    — did not supply it in circumstances such that the relevant person is entitled apart from these Regulations to disclose it, and
    — has not consented to its disclosure, or
- the disclosure of the information in response to that request would, in the circumstances, increase the likelihood of damage to the environment affecting anything to which the information relates.

The Regulations permit charges in respect of costs reasonably attributable to the supply of information, provided a schedule of the charges that may be levied is made available to all persons requesting environmental information. There is no upper cost limit in the regulations.

Table 7.1 highlights the key differences between the Regulations and FOI.

Table 7.1 Freedom of Information Act (FOI) and Environmental Information Regulations (EIRs): key differences between the regimes (*Reproduced with kind permission of Public Partners*)

FOI regime	EIR regime
1 FOI concerns all recorded information held by public authorities.	EIRs concern all recorded environmental information held by public authorities. The definition of public authorities in this context might also include private sector organizations who provide public services or exercise public functions under the control of a public body.

Continued on next page

Table 7.1 *Continued*

FOI regime	EIR regime
2 FOI requests must be made in writing.	EIR requests can be made in writing but do not have to be. They can also be made orally: in person or over the telephone.
3 The term used under FOI for information that is not releasable under the Act is 'exemption'.	Exemptions in the EIRs are called exceptions.
4 A FOI request can be refused if an exemption applies. However, with many (but not all) exemptions, there is a further requirement to consider whether the public interest in disclosing exempt information is greater than the public interest in withholding it.	An EIR request can be refused if an exception applies. EIR exceptions cover the same ground as FOI exemptions but there are two key differences: • Under the EIRs the public interest test applies to all exceptions including statute bars. • An exception cannot usually be claimed if the information is about emissions.
5 There is a cost limit. This is likely to be £550.	No cost limit is specified in the EIRs and cost is not a sufficient reason for refusing to find and provide the information.
6 Public authorities have 20 working days to answer a FOI request. Where the information is exempt and a public interest test is required, there is a further unspecified period in which to do this. The initial reply to the applicant (within the 20 working days) must say how long the public interest test will take.	A 20-working-day deadline is specified in the EIRs for straightforward requests for environmental information and the public interest test must be done within this period. However, a further 20 working days is allowed to answer very complicated or high volume queries, although an initial reply must be sent within 20 working days.

Other legislation

Numerous other enactments may influence the operation of freedom of information. At the time of writing the Department for Constitutional Affairs is examining over 200 Acts of Parliament to establish the effect that the FOI Act has on them. This process will lead to the repeal of some of that legislation. Other Acts will have precedence over the Freedom of Information Act.

Some of the enactments cited in Chapter 1 are likely to remain. To these one might add the Limitation Act 1980 which, while not having a direct bearing on freedom of information, affects the periods for which many records will need to be retained. In essence public authorities need to undertake a risk assessment, identifying for themselves what the risks are of destroying certain information and having to entertain a claim for compensation or damages for which that information would be required. Requests for information from records retained or destroyed in this way may be made. There should be no worries for public authorities as long as the records have been destroyed in accordance with an established policy and that fact is recorded.

Notes

1   Section 68 defines an accessible record as a health record, an educational
    record or an accessible public record. These are defined in great detail in
    the Data Protection Act 1998.

2   Apart from Regulation 3(7) which states: 'Subject to regulation 4 below
    [this regulation on confidential information], where any statutory provi-
    sion or rule of law imposes any restriction or prohibition on the disclosure
    of information by any person, that restriction or prohibition shall not
    apply to any disclosure of information in pursuance of these Regulations.'

8

Staffing and training

This chapter examines the roles of the staff who will be required to manage an organization's records and information. It provides a detailed framework of the skills and knowledge required by such staff, and gives examples of training programmes.

Staffing

Freedom of Information

The infrastructure for implementing Freedom of Information needs to be in place well before January 2005.

To a large extent the staffing organization will depend on two factors:

- the size of the organization
- the likely number of requests.

Every public authority, however, must have one person in overall charge of discharging the freedom of information function – the freedom of information officer. The most efficient way of dealing with requests for information is likely to be for answers to be provided by appropriate operational or business units. This means, of course, that the freedom of information officer must have contacts in each of those areas. They may be responsible for answering requests and giving advice on the application of the exemptions. This is likely to be a full-time occupation in most medium-to-large public authorities but perhaps a part-time post in smaller organizations. It is important, given the time restraints on answering requests for information, that these contacts have an appointed deputy.

The staff in the operational units must also have regard to the operation of the authority's publication scheme. They must, in conjunction with the freedom of information officer, ensure that the scheme is up to date and that requests for information from it are met within a reasonable time. The freedom of information officer would normally be responsible for ensuring that access to the scheme is available to all (including those without electronic means) and for liaising with the Office of the Information Commissioner on changes to or approvals of the scheme.

Records management

The Code of Practice under section 46 of the Act requires all public authorities to have a records manager. Larger organizations will also have records management staff. Much work has been done over the past few years in identifying skills and knowledge required in the records management function. A competency framework produced by the National Archives in 2001 has much to commend it.

Competency framework *Reproduced with kind permission of the National Archives*

Records managers, their staff and all who are concerned with the management of information need to develop particular knowledge and skills in order to meet these challenges, to ensure the effective operation of their organizations and businesses, to provide the means for achieving corporate objectives, and to contribute to the Government's overall policy of modernizing the public service.

This section consists of three distinctive but interrelated elements:

* a competency framework
* job and person specifications
* training and development.

The competency framework has been developed to help define the 'people capability' required in records management organizations. The competencies are set in a framework of four descriptive levels which relate closely to the grouping of work in records management units. The competencies themselves, however, may be utilized in various ways when applied to an organization, depending on a number of factors: its functions, its size, information and corporate strategies, and the level of information technology it uses. The levels do not correspond to grading; for example, a senior member of staff may have a low requirement for some of the functional competencies but a very high requirement for the managerial competencies.

The job and person specifications section includes definitions and examples which, in conjunction with the competency framework, will provide the means for describing roles at the different levels of records management work. These may range from the head of a large information services organization to records support staff in a small operational unit. The specifications have been created as examples and are not representative of any existing organization.

The guidance also contains information on training and development which may need to be introduced as a result of a competency assessment arising from the framework and specifications outlined above.

Competencies

Competencies describe what people do in the workplace at various levels and specify the standards for each of those levels; they identify the characteristics, knowledge and skills possessed or required by individuals that enable them to undertake their duties and responsibilities effectively and thus to achieve professional quality standards in their work; and they cover all aspects of records management performance – particular skills and knowledge, attitudes, communication, application and development. Three kinds of competency are used in this framework:

- core competencies – relate to a records management organization's strategic priorities and values; applicable to all records management staff
- managerial competencies – reflect the managerial activity and performance required in certain records management roles
- functional competencies – describe the role-specific abilities required; usually relate to professional or technical skills.

Levels of knowledge/expertise

The framework uses four levels of competencies:

- learner – requires some support; just beginning to need to demonstrate the competency
- threshold – able to perform most aspects of a competency without supervision
- excellent – consistently demonstrates very good performance in most aspects of the competency; coaching others in the competency is an important part of this level
- expert – demonstrates outstanding performance in a competency at a complex level; viewed as superior by others (within the organization and outside it); creates the environment in which others can succeed in the competency.

Framework

The framework is prefaced by a list of the competencies in the three categories of core, managerial and functional. Each one of these competencies is then described at the four levels of learner, threshold, excellent and expert. The descriptions for each level are examples of the skills or knowledge that should be reached before qualifying for the particular level. In the case of the core and managerial competencies these descriptions might be considered as relatively standard across a particular part of the public sector. The functional competencies, however, may be dependent on the strategic objectives and organizational management of particular organizations. The framework is set out on pages 116-28.

Application of the framework

Each role in a records management unit can be described in terms of a 'competency profile' which indicates:

• the competencies required in the job (selected from the framework)
• the level of a competency which must be demonstrated in that job.

The framework is a tool that organizations can use or adapt to draw up their own role profiles. It can also be used to identify training and development needs, by assessing staff against role profiles, and to define the competencies required when recruiting new staff. Competency frameworks and role profiles work best when they are tailored to a particular organization. In this respect the framework offered here should serve as an effective starting point.

A senior member of staff should take responsibility for the framework and ensure that it is maintained and kept up to date in the light of experience and developments in records management. It is suggested that revisions should happen at least once every six months.

Example of a profile: records manager

Role: develop and manage an organization-wide records management programme designed to ensure that records practices are effectively meeting the organization's objectives.

Competency	Level
Knowledge and history of the organization	3
Knowledge of the [sectoral] environment	3
Professionalism	3
Communication and marketing	3
Teamworking	2
Planning and time management	3
IT literacy	2
Flexibility	3
Customer care	3
Coaching and development	3
Influencing	3
Advice and guidance	3

Continued on next page

Competency	Level
Manage performance	3
Manage people	2
Manage projects	3
Maintaining standards	3
Administration	2
Information management	2
Information technology	1
Information policy	3
Records management and archival practice	3
Specialist knowledge	3

Job and person specifications

The specifications are designed principally to aid managers in the recruitment of suitable staff to records management units. They can, however, also be used as a basis for performance management plans with staff at the beginning of each business year and, in conjunction with performance assessments, may be used to identify training and development requirements.

Role types

Roles in records management may be said to be of four main types:

- director of information services – the post that oversees the information management function in an organization, usually including IT and information management responsibility; their main role is the formulation of policy and contribution to the achievement of the organization's corporate objectives by ensuring that it raises the standard of records and information management, including electronic records
- records manager/departmental records officer – the post which has direct managerial responsibility for the records management function, including the management and appraisal of electronic records
- records executive – typically the records executive or records supervisor will take charge of specific areas of records management within the overall management of an organization's records and information; for example, they may be responsible for all matters concerning the management of active records – file classification systems, inspection of file management units, or liaison with nominated officers throughout the organization; they may take charge of an organization's intermediate records and be responsible for the operation of an appraisal system

- records assistant – the post of records assistant may be used in a number of ways; for example, preparing records for transfer to an archive, retrieving and replacing records for the organization's own staff, compiling lists and other finding aids to selected records.

Job specifications

A job specification should comprise two main elements: purpose and description.

Purpose of the job

The purpose of the job consists of a short statement outlining the main components of a particular role. These will underpin the job holder's performance management plan and contribute to departmental and corporate objectives.

Examples of the purpose of a job

- be responsible for the management and use of departmental information and administrative services, including strategic planning and information technology
- develop and manage an organization-wide records management programme designed to ensure that records practices are effectively meeting the organization's needs
- oversee all activities pertaining to the management of non-current records, including receipt, storage, retrieval, review and disposal
- assist in the provision of an efficient records management system and mail processing system to service the whole of the organization's operations.

Job description

The job description lists the particular duties and responsibilities of the role.

Job description: example 1

- create, manage, control and direct the records and information management programme for the whole department
- direct the development of records and information policies and procedures
- undertake the role of information strategist, determining staffing, equipment and other resources required to meet corporate objectives
- be responsible for financial planning of records and information services.

Job description: example 2

- establish procedures and direct the implementation of the records management programme

- monitor compliance with legislative and other record-keeping requirements
- develop record-keeping and records management standards and rules, including those for electronic record-keeping
- provide technical support and co-ordination of personnel resources necessary for the successful operation of the programme
- provide technical training to business unit records personnel as required
- be responsible for addressing and resolving issues within the records management areas
- be responsible to the Information Services Director for the records management budget and cost control
- establish procedures for the evaluation, development and review of manual and automated records systems
- design and implement effective records disposal schemes
- advise on and implement effective strategies for storage of active records (electronic and paper)
- manage an off-site storage programme for inactive records
- prepare periodic reports for the Information Services Director with respect to the records management operations.

Job description: example 3

- supervise and co-ordinate the work of the records centre staff
- develop and supervise training programmes for records centre staff and for user departments to ensure consistency and standardization
- develop and implement policies and procedures for the records centre
- undertake special research requests from user departments
- ensure the application of disposal schedules
- ensure efficient utilization of storage space
- ensure security and preservation of the records in the records centre
- ensure that records are produced to user departments when requested and within agreed timescales
- liaise with the PRO Client Manager on review procedures
- prepare reports on the maintenance, use and disposal of non-current records.

Job description: example 4

- account for the accurate recording of file data and movement of files throughout the organization
- make files available on demand
- circulate files to officers in accordance with established procedures
- provide assistance and information on status of files
- collect and distribute outward mail
- process inward mail

- establish and maintain property series files under the direction of the Records Manager
- assist with co-ordination of copier maintenance
- assist with file courier service as required.

Person specification

The person specification draws directly on the competency framework. It specifies those skills required for the job and the level at which they should be pitched. For example, the role described in example 1 might require the following person specification:

- qualifications – honours degree, or at least five years' experience in senior management
- experience – an understanding of organizational structures and policy-making processes; an awareness of records management principles and practices
- skills – high level of interpersonal skills; ability to work as part of a team; initiative; decisiveness; consistency.

The role described in example 2 above might have the following person specification:

- qualifications – tertiary qualifications in records management
- experience – five years' records management experience, ideally in a supervisory role; experience in implementing and maintaining a computer-based records system desirable
- specialist skills and knowledge – computer keyboard skills; knowledge of activities and operations of government; understanding of archives legislation
- management skills – ability to work within specified timescales to achieve set objectives
- interpersonal skills – ability to liaise with staff at all levels and assist them in records and research functions; essential to work in a team environment to achieve a team objective.

Training and development

The issues surrounding the demand for more efficient and reliable management of information and the automation of business give rise to training and development needs across the public sector. The competency framework detailed earlier and the job and person specifications linked to it provide the means to identify those needs. They are also a powerful tool in supporting accreditations such as Investors in People.

The framework can be used for long-term development by:

- planning and providing for the development of appropriate and relevant transferable skills and knowledge
- assisting with performance management, by identifying and linking relevant competencies and competency levels to individual jobs
- helping with succession planning by providing for the identification and measurement of the minimum competencies and competency levels required at different levels of appointment.

Staff development must be seen in conjunction with the operational needs of organizations. In the records management function these are set out in legislation, standards and best practice guidelines, but they will also be integrated closely with the work and strategic priorities of the organization as a whole.

Training and development in records management require commitment on the part of organizations, particularly in planning the development of employees on the basis of competency assessment and action to implement the plans. This would be followed by an evaluation of the results of the training in order to assess achievement and improve future effectiveness.

Development plan

Each member of the records management function should have a development plan, drawn up on the basis of a comparison between their skills and the competencies necessary for their role. Such a plan should be guided by the organization's strategic priorities. The plan should be drawn up at the beginning of each business year, in conjunction with the performance management plan for the individual. It should identify the skills which are to be developed, the methods used to develop them, the contribution that this development will make to the organization's corporate objectives, and criteria for the evaluation of the success of the development activity. The plan should be reviewed and evaluated regularly during the year to assess progress in achieving its objectives.

Development might be undertaken in a number of different ways:

- reading
- videos and electronic learning materials
- mentoring and coaching
- formal courses
- on-the-job learning.

Training methods should be chosen to suit the individual involved and the learning objectives.

Example of a development plan:

Name   Department

Date   Job Title

Objective *What is my aim?*	Linked to *Why am I doing it?*	Method *How am I going to do it?*	Measures *How will I measure my progress?*	Date of Completion of Objective	Support/ coaches *What help do I need?*

Records Management Competency Framework

Core competencies

- Knowledge and history of the organization
- Knowledge of the [sectoral] environment
- Professionalism
- Communication and promoting records management
- Teamworking
- Planning and time management
- IT literacy
- Flexibility
- Customer care/client focus

Managerial competencies

- Coaching and development
- Influencing
- Managing performance
- Maintaining standards
- Managing people
- Managing projects

Continued on next page

Functional competencies

- Information policy
- Information management
- Information technology
- Records management and archival practice
- Administration
- Specialist knowledge

Core competencies

Level	Description
Knowledge and history of the organization	
1	• Has a basic understanding of the function and role of the organization, both past and present, and can explain this to others • Is familiar with the structure of the organization.
2	• Understands the remit afforded to the organization by legislation, both past and present. • Understands the different record-keeping and referencing systems used by the organization over the past 25 years or more and can explain them to others. • Is aware of the high-profile subjects covered by the organization and their implications for records work.
3	• Understands and acts on implications of past and present processes in the department, including the review and selection of records. • Explains and advises on the changes in the organization's role and responsibilities over the past few years and the documentary evidence supporting them.
4	• Envisages the future role of records within the organization. • Coaches colleagues in developing their knowledge and understanding of the organization both past and present.
Knowledge of the government* environment	
1	• Understands how the department fits into the government framework.
2	• Understands how the policy process works. • Is aware of the implications of government information policy on records work and can explain this to others. • Demonstrates own knowledge of government environment in decision making. • Demonstrates a knowledge of modern British history.

Continued on next page

Level	Description
3	• Is able to identify records implications of new government policy. • Actively improves own understanding of the machinery of government and the decision-making process.
4	• Understands changes in status and structure of government, government departments and social factors, and analyses impact on the department. • Is able to influence the policy process outside the department. • Is seen by others as an expert source of advice within the department on the machinery of government and modern British administrative history. • Coaches colleagues to generate greater insight into government roles and organization.

*Government used as an example of a particular section.

Professionalism

1	• Creates a positive impression of the section with clients. • Is delivery focused. • Responds promptly to requests for advice. • Refers questions to experts and ensures that action is taken to resolve issues.
2	• Provides objective professional advice to clients. • Communicates records policy consistently to clients and colleagues. • Has a confident approach in the application of records management. • Seeks to maintain current level of expertise.
3	• Demonstrates relevant expertise and applies this consistently in records work. • Is up to date with developments in own field of expertise and applies this in own work. • Takes ownership of client issues and ensures their successful resolution. • Deals confidently with senior managers in other divisions. • Coaches others in developing more professional standards.
4	• Initiates records policy. • Informs records policy with best practice approach. • Role models standards to colleagues.

Continued on next page

Level	Description
Communication and promoting records management	
1	• Is clear and precise in written and oral communication. • Can make simple presentations. • Makes best use of available means of communication.
2	• Communicates effectively to different audiences. • Generates interest and enthusiasm in others. • Translates technical terms into formats appropriate for their audience.
3	• Develops opportunities for raising the profile of records management. • Produces effective communication and marketing plans. • Can assimilate and disseminate complex information. • Is able to interpret a brief, and create and deliver an effective presentation to large groups.
4	• Is an effective and inspirational speaker. • Is persuasive and influential when conversing with others. • Enhances communication and marketing through the development and implementation of communication and marketing strategies.
Teamworking	
1	• Provides support for colleagues on own initiative. • Understands own and others' roles within the team. • Recognizes the need for teamwork.
2	• Energetically pursues team targets. • Willingly undertakes different team roles. • Forms good working relationships with other teams.
3	• Builds team effectiveness. • Sets and communicates direction for a team. • Generates enthusiasm for team and individual goals.
4	• Is able to select team members according to business needs and individual development requirements. • Role models team working. • Identifies and manages the collective responsibility of the team. • Aims to develop the team's collective ability.

Continued on next page

Level	Description

Planning and time management

1	• Completes tasks allocated on time.
	• Understands the scarcity of the time resource and the requirement to manage it.
	• Prioritizes according to organizational policy.
	• Manages conflicting priorities in own work.
2	• Plans and manages own workload to ensure completion.
	• Monitors progress against targets and takes corrective action when required.
	• Accurately plans out activities according to workload requirements.
	• Works methodically.
3	• Ensures that resources within a project or task are best deployed to meet targets.
	• Delegates tasks effectively to others and ensures that they have the skills to succeed.
	• Uses past experience to inform project planning and work allocation.
	• Resolves priority conflicts for team members.
4	• Allocates assignments in the most efficient way.
	• Recognizes the importance of making personal time available for individual person management.
	• Generates options to address resource issues.
	• Is solutions-focused.

IT literacy

1	• Demonstrates basic knowledge of relevant IT packages and systems.*
	• Uses this knowledge to perform own work efficiently.
2	• Demonstrates good knowledge of relevant IT packages and systems.*
	• Actively seeks to extend competency in information systems.
3	• Is able to use relevant specialist software in the organization.
	• Is able to use records management software packages.
	• Coaches colleagues in the use of software and hardware.
4	• Identifies requirements for new, or new versions of, software applications.
	• Maintains a good level of knowledge of IT developments.
	• Advises colleagues on IT issues.

* Relevant IT packages and systems cover: word processing; spreadsheets; databases; e-mail; internet.

Continued on next page

Level	Description
Flexibility	
1	• Is willing to accept changes to job content. • Adapts personal schedule to meet critical demands and to support colleagues. • Is responsive to client and/or client needs.
2	• Moves willingly between different jobs. • Works easily with different people. • Displays ability to apply policy flexibly. • Works effectively in a changing environment.
3	• Initiates and manages change. • Is professionally innovative. • Demonstrates ability to alter management style to suit different situations. • Is results-orientated.
4	• Role models and encourages flexibility in others. • Creates a flexible culture for others. • Seeks to improve performance and the working environment through change and innovation.
Customer care/client focus	
1	• Understands the importance of ongoing customer care. • Adjusts personal style to deal with different customers. • Recognizes the importance of service levels.
2	• Builds relationships at a number of different levels in a customer's organization. • Understands clients' needs. • Has systematic contact with customers on a regular basis. • Formulates and manages service-level agreements with customers.
3	• Actively solicits feedback from customers. • Ensures continuity of service levels through mentoring and coaching. • Makes every effort to ensure that customers have the necessary resources to meet required records management standards. • Monitors service levels for a number of customers and deals with conflicting demands. • Provides expertise and coaches others in customer care.

Continued on next page

Level	Description
4	• Develops policies for achieving close and effective relationships with customers. • Actively develops relationships with customers at a senior level. • Seeks and uses feedback from customers to improve customer care.

Managerial competencies

Coaching and development

1	• Takes personal responsibility for own development. • Continuously improves personal competence in line with requirements of own job and career aspirations. • Regularly seeks feedback on personal performance.
2	• Regularly discusses training and development needs with staff, linking them with individual and team business targets. • Identifies and agrees training and development needs and ensures that they are met. • Actively supports staff throughout the training process, by briefing and debriefing, and provides information about available training.
3	• Identifies potential and expertise in others. • Measures and evaluates impact of training and development initiatives. • Ensures individuals' knowledge is shared and captured.
4	• Creates and encourages a culture of knowledge sharing within the organization. • Creates opportunities to enhance learning and knowledge across the organization. • Identifies and implements career development opportunities for staff.

Influencing

1	• Is able to identify the benefits of records management policies. • Is assertive with others in ensuring understanding of key information. • Understands and can apply own influencing styles.
2	• Is able to describe to others the benefits of changing records management practices. • Is able to utilize a range of persuasion techniques. • Understands how to influence others. • Recognizes when to be assertive to achieve results.

Continued on next page

Level	Description
3	• Is able to change existing records management behaviours. • Is able to moderate personal style with others to maximize outcomes. • Is able to create change in records management policies throughout the organization.
4	• Facilitates inter-departmental debates on records management best practice. • Coaches others in developing their influencing skills. • Works to ensure that the records section is closely involved in the departmental decision-making process.

Managing performance

Level	Description
1	• Contributes to the achievement of individual and team targets. • Monitors own performance on a regular basis.
2	• Identifies potential risks to performance achievement and responds promptly. • Sets clear and achievable team targets and objectives, and manages their successful achievement. • Understands how processes underlie performance.
3	• Uses resources to maximize cost effectiveness of service provision. • Consistently delivers targets within budget and provides accurate management information. • Is able to develop corporate and business plans with useful measures of performance.
4	• Manages collective performance to achieve business priorities and objectives. • Allocates and manages resources to ensure the achievement of business priorities and objectives. • Manages risk in order to maintain performance levels. • Encourages others to initiate change to improve performance.

Maintaining standards

Level	Description
1	• Understands and communicates the need for quality standards. • Is able to identify and implement ideas for improved quality of service in own work. • Consistently applies records management standards.

Continued on next page

Level	Description
2	• Implements changes to quality standards. • Is able to identify and implement ideas for improved quality of performance. • Recognizes resource constraints in achieving quality standards.
3	• Generates standards to meet organizational needs. • Promotes quality improvement throughout the organization. • Seeks feedback on overall quality of service. • Monitors standards and provides management information as required.
4	• Promotes quality improvements in records management. • Creates a culture that promotes the need for standards. • Ensures availability of accurate quality information for management reporting.

Managing people

1	• Manages self and others in the completion of a task. • Represents the needs of colleagues to superiors. • Understands the performance management system and ensures that own contribution is valid. • Demonstrates commitment to personal development.
2	• Recognizes and rewards good performance both formally and informally. • Reviews individual and team performance and provides feedback. • Forms effective working relationships. • Delegates effectively to others.
3	• Creates and communicates direction in a clear and consistent way. • Enhances productive working relationships. • Consults and communicates with others in areas of joint interest. • Provides effective change management.
4	• Creates an environment in which people are motivated and inspired. • Creates a culture where individuals and teams own the impact of their actions. • Provides leadership and direction during change.

Managing projects

1	• Can plan and deliver simple projects. • Monitors progress against objectives. • Understands basic project management techniques.

Continued on next page

Level	Description
2	• Identifies project objectives, risks and success factors. • Delivers projects according to time, cost and quality targets. • Takes action where progress is not in line with objectives. • Understands and can apply a range of project management techniques. • Manages suppliers on a day-to-day basis.
3	• Manages complex or multiple projects. • Manages contracts with external suppliers. • Identifies in advance potential risks and their solutions. • Creates, develops and manages project teams. • Is able to negotiate satisfactory contracts with suppliers.
4	• Is seen by others as an expert in project management. • Generates, communicates and maintains a best practice project management model. • Ensures deliverables are in line with business strategies.

Functional competencies

Information management

1	• Recognizes and understands the differences between various types of electronic records and the systems which produce them.
2	• Is able to supervise the inventory and audit of electronic records assemblies. • Is able to provide advice on the development and application of procedures for managing electronic records.
3	• Advises colleagues on mapping the information flows between different systems and putting the information in a business context; assesses the implications of new systems development on electronic and paper records. • Actively encourages colleagues to use and manage records as information assets. • Contributes to the development of corporate records policies.
4	• Develops an understanding of information policy and its implications for electronic records. • Develops and maintains outside contacts to keep abreast of information management issues and techniques. • Generates new and innovative approaches to tackling information management issues.

Continued on next page

Level	Description

Information technology

1	• Has a basic knowledge of software and hardware applications and their usage in the organization.
2	• Has practical experience of software/systems design and the provision of ongoing support. • Is able to generate solutions to ensure the continuing integrity of data held by the organization.
3	• Is able to develop an IT strategy for records and to contribute to organization-wide IT strategies. • Demonstrates an awareness of leading edge developments in IT. • Is able to implement an electronic document management system. • Understands the implications of related office systems, such as workflow and image processing, for records management systems. • Liaises with relevant IT specialists in government and industry.
4	• Generates approaches to electronic records management issues emerging from IT strategies. • Challenges and develops others' knowledge of IT systems and developments.

Information policy

1	• Understands and can explain to others the implications of the organization's information policy. • Continuously develops own understanding of the information policy.
2	• Facilitates liaison with other information professionals. • Demonstrates awareness of issues relating to the management of current information. • Understands the implications of Data Protection and Freedom of Information legislation and can interpret and apply relevant guidelines.
3	• Contributes to the development of responses to changes in information policy. • Ensures that own reports show awareness of changes in information policy.
4	• Is consulted as an expert on information policy. • Provides guidance and advice on the implications of Data Protection and Freedom of Information. • Develops organizational information policy and expertise.

Continued on next page

Level	Description

Records management and archival practice

Level	Description
1	• Is aware of different records media and associated records management implications. • Has a basic knowledge of document preservation and repair techniques. • Demonstrates knowledge of packaging, transfer and storage techniques.
2	• Is able to interpret and apply guidelines on the management of conventional and electronic records. • Follows best practice principles in managing records. • Demonstrates knowledge of records legislation.
3	• Seeks to think creatively about the records management and archival process. • Has a knowledge of other records repositories and their specialisms. • Applies records management standards and best practice guidelines in storing, appraising and selecting appropriate records.
4	• Develops records management policies which reflect best practice and legislative environment. • Is seen as an expert on records management and archives administration within the organization and by external bodies. • Uses experience and knowledge to coach others in records management. • Is involved with external bodies in the further development of best practice in records management and archives administration.

Administration

Level	Description
1	• Administers simple tasks successfully and learns from mistakes. • Follows procedures. • Is able to use basic office equipment. • Respects and maintains the confidential nature of records and information entrusted to them. • Pays attention to detail.
2	• Checks for accuracy in other people's work. • Creates and administers simple budgets. • Administers complex tasks successfully. • Maintains an effective filing system. • Works within agreed procedures.

Continued on next page

Level	Description
3	• Initiates invoices. • Demonstrates a basic working knowledge of procurement and contract management. • Works within and monitors procedures.
4	• Allocates administrative tasks across team members. • Monitors the administration of a number of complex tasks.

Specialist knowledge*

1	• Demonstrates a basic knowledge of the subject. • Is able to access sources for more information/greater detail.
2	• Demonstrates a good knowledge of the subject, both in theory and application. • Is able to apply knowledge to current working environment.
3	• Demonstrates an in-depth subject knowledge. • Provides relevant and helpful advice to others. • Shares knowledge willingly.
4	• Demonstrates a subject knowledge in breadth and depth. • Is seen as an expert and consulted by others regularly.

* Specialist knowledge might include: understanding of statistical research and sampling techniques; knowledge of particular types of records; specialist IT knowledge.

Training

It is essential that everyone working in a public authority who is likely to be in the business of providing information is familiar with the requirements of the Act and with the Codes of Practice. Indeed, since a request for information could in theory be handed to anyone in a public authority, it would be as well that everyone in the authority is aware of what they need to do in such a circumstance. Public authorities should therefore ensure that proper training is provided. The training will need to take regard of other provisions which may affect the implementation of freedom of information, such as the Data Protection Act 1998 and the Environmental Information Regulations.

Training needs to be built into the routine activity of an organization. It may take various forms:

- induction training – where new entrants are made aware not only of their responsibilities to record their actions and decisions in the discharge of their functions but also of the general requirements of the Freedom of Information Act

- handling requests – the staffing infrastructure for implementing freedom of information must be settled at an early stage and training of the personnel involved undertaken; the person in overall charge of the FOI function (probably called the freedom of information officer) will need specialist training to ensure that they are well versed in all aspects and nuances of the legislation and of related provisions
- disclosure decisions – staff in specialist areas may be called upon to give advice on the application or otherwise of exemptions; they will need to be aware of the deadlines involved as well as the exemption and public interest aspects of the legislation
- records management – records managers and those in related functions (such as archivists and knowledge managers) must know the Code of Practice under section 46 of the Act; they should also be aware of the general requirements of the legislation
- finance – financial managers will be called upon to make provision for various initiatives under the Act; this may range from resources for training to the implementation of an electronic records management system, and may include a FOI tracking system, extra staff and extra accommodation (for both public and staff)
- trainers – public authorities may decide to buy in training expertise or they may decide to train their own trainers
- information technology – IT has an important role to play in freedom of information; tracking systems and records management systems will need to be maintained and provide an effective service; given the deadlines imposed by the Act these systems cannot afford to be inoperative for too long; IT staff will need to understand the Act and what it means for their function within the authority.

The following outlines are examples of training to:

- give an overview of freedom of information
- implement an action plan for developing records management

and can be downloaded ready for use as a Powerpoint presentation at www. facetpublishing.co.uk/foi.

Overview of freedom of information

Reproduced with kind permission of the National Archives

What does FOI mean for the public?

- An opportunity to find out what publicly funded bodies do and how they do it
- An opportunity to make these bodies more accountable
- Primarily aimed at current information but applies also to archives

The rights of access

- Right of access to recorded information held by public authorities, irrespective of its age
- Any letter or email is a potential FOI request for information
- 20 working days to confirm or deny information is held and provide it, unless an exemption applies
- Duty to provide advice and assistance

Some terms explained

- **Public authorities**
  - Public sector plus and minus
- **Information**
  - Current
  - Archives
- **Irrespective of age**
  - 30 year closure period goes
  - Concept of 'historical records'

Fees

- **FOI Fees Regulations set fee to be charged**
  - 10% cost of finding information
  - 0% cost of making disclosure decision
  - 100% actual costs of release eg copies
- **Alternative fees regime may be used – but only if statutory**

Publication schemes

- **Schemes are to promote pro-active release of information so that rights of access become a fall-back**
- **Approved scheme must be in place by deadline for each sector**
- **Schemes contain promises that must be kept – embed in administrative procedures**
- **Enforceable by Information Commissioner**

What should a scheme contain?

- Introduction or foreword
- list of classes of information - but exclude exempt information
- Details of when & how to be released
- Details of any charges to apply
- Cover archives & finding aids
- Guidance available
  - OIC website
  - model schemes, templates
  - Places of deposit Bulletin

Get-out exemptions

- **Cost limit (s 12) – limit set in Fees Regulations**
- **Information is already or about to be already reasonably accessible (s 21 – s 22)**
  - Accessible through publication scheme – could include archives in a search room or on internet
  - Accessible because of another Act

Content exemptions

- **Class-based, eg**
  - Court records, honours & awards,
- **Prejudice tested, eg**
  - Defence, law enforcement, commercial interests, physical or mental health, safety
- **Some sunset provisions, ie exemptions expire at 30, 60 or 100 years (see s 63 – s 64)**

Go-to-another-regime exemptions

- **Environmental information(s 39)**
  - EI Regulations
- **Personal information about the applicant (s 40(1))**
  - Data Protection Act - data subject access
  - Note that FOI extends the DP Act to personal information in unstructured manual files

3rd party access to personal information

- **Data subject alive**
  - do not disclose if Data Protection Principles would be breached
- **Data subject dead**
  - Disclose unless another exemption applies
    - physical or mental health or safety
    - conferring of honours or awards
    - Information supplied in confidence

Public interest test

- **With some exemptions, must consider the public interest in disclosing exempt information, eg**
  - Commercial interests, honours & awards,
- **Other exemptions are 'absolute', ie no public interest test, eg**
  - Court records, information supplied in confidence

Codes of practice

- **Section 45 code - handling of requests, public sector contracts, internal review of complaints**
- **Section 46 code**
  - Part I - records management
  - Part II – review and transfer of public records
- **Enforcement by Information Commissioner**

Enforcement

- **Information Commissioner and Information Tribunal**
- **Information Notices**
- **Decision Notices**
- **Practice Recommendations**
- **Consultation with Keeper of Public Records re s 46 code in public record bodies**

Section 45 code and enquiry procedures

- **Publish request procedures**
- **Types of assistance to offer**
- **Transferring requests**
- **Consulting 3rd parties**
- **Public sector contracts**
- **Complaints procedure**

Disclosure decisions

- **What is involved?**
  - application of exemption
  - public interest test
  - confirm or deny information is held?
- **Who makes the decision?**
- **Who is consulted about the decision?**

Calculating fees

- **Expected provisions:**
  - 10% cost of finding information
  - 0% cost of making disclosure decision
  - 100% cost of copies etc
  - cost limit of £500
- **How much does it cost to find information in archives?**

Managing requests for information

- Logging
- Tracking progress against deadline
- Decision-making
- Documenting

Conclusion

- Plan
- Read guidance
- Think hard
- Network and collaborate
- Don't panic

Developing records management

Reproduced with kind permission of the National Archives

Why RM matters for FOI

- Do you know what information you hold and where it is?
- If information has been destroyed, can you show when and why?
- Are you keeping the records you need for current and future information and evidence purposes?

FOI Act s. 46 (1)

The Lord Chancellor shall issue, and may from time to time revise, a code of practice providing guidance to relevant authorities as to the practice which it would, in his opinion, be desirable for them to follow in connection with the keeping, management and destruction of their records.

Preface

*iii)   Any freedom of information legislation is only as good as the quality of the records to which it provides access.........................
....................Consequently, all public authorities are encouraged to pay heed to the guidance in the Code.*

Model Action Plans

- Advisory Group on Openness in the Public Sector (December 1999)
- Model action plan for developing records management compliant with the Code of Practice
  - Central Government
  - Local Government
  - FE and HE
  - Police
  - NHS, Schools......

Nine Steps

- The Records Management Function
- Records Manager
- Policy Statement
- Training and Awareness
- Record Creation and Keeping
- Record Maintenance
- Record Disposal
- Access
- Performance Management

**Step 1
The Records Management Function**

- specific corporate programme
- organisational support
- records in all formats
- clearly defined responsibilities
- connection with other information management issues

Step 2
Roles and Responsibilities

- records manager
- appropriate skills and knowledge
- appropriate resources
- analysis of training needs

Step 3

6.1 *An authority should have in place an overall policy statement, endorsed by top management and made readily available to staff at all levels of the organisation, on how it manages its records, including electronic records.*

Step 3 - contd

" mandate for all records management functions
" commitment to create, keep and manage records
" role of records management
" relationship to overall strategy
" roles and responsibilities
" framework for supporting standards, procedures and guidelines
" monitor compliance
" reviewed at regular intervals (at least once every three years)

Step 4
Training and Awareness

- records management awareness
- professional development programme

Step 5
Record Creation and Record Keeping

- adequate system for documenting activities
- complete and accurate
- quick and easy retrieval
- information survey/record audit
- metadata
- rules of description

Step 6
Record Maintenance

" tracking system
" adequate storage
" suitable equipment
" handling procedures
" business recovery plan

Step 7
Record Disposal

- closure procedures
- standards for the storage of closed records
- volume and nature of records due for disposal
- time taken to appraise
- risk management
- documentation system
- acquisition and disposition policies
- operational selection policy
- disposal schedules
- destruction

Step 8
Access

- Documentation of disclosure and exemption decisions

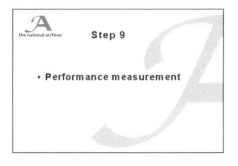

Public authorities should not forget that the public need to be made aware of freedom of information and about the way that public authorities will handle enquiries. While the Information Commissioner has prime responsibility for this, the duty to provide advice and assistance means that authorities should consider issuing leaflets and guides to members of the public. They must inform applicants for information of the complaints and appeal procedures but a more active dissemination of guidance will benefit both the public and the authority.

Authorities might also consider the role that the media will play in the implementation of freedom of information. Journalists are likely to be an active group when the Act becomes fully operational. Involving the media in operations will help to increase public awareness and ease any future applications for information that they may make.

Finally, monitoring the effectiveness of training and awareness should be undertaken. Feedback from recipients and networking with participants will help to ensure that the training is achieving its objectives.

9

Getting ready for Freedom of Information

This chapter brings together all the elements of previous chapters into a practical plan for the implementation of the provisions of the FOI Act, concluding with a sample plan of a typical project.

There are eight major steps that need to be taken to be ready for the implementation of Freedom of Information.

1 Planning

Implementing Freedom of Information policies and procedures can be regarded as a discrete project and the preferred methodology brought to it. Since, from the time of writing, the legislation will come fully into force in a matter of months (1 January 2005), many public authorities will already have a project under way. If not, there is no time to lose. It should be set in motion now.

There are three essential elements to the planning phase:

- communication
- volume
- resources.

Communication

Everyone in the organization needs to know about the introduction of the new legislation and what their responsibilities might be. This may range from simply knowing where to pass on requests for information to being responsible for making disclosure decisions. Whatever it is, letting people know is vital. Communication should come from the top and should be kept active by the project manager. Make use of all available vehicles – newsletters, intranet, regular meetings, circulars, etc.

Support and leadership at a senior level in an authority is vital. With this in place the organization will be able to achieve the real change – particularly cultural change – that is necessary for the effective implementation of FOI. Many authorities have already appointed a member of staff at management board level to champion the cause of Freedom of Information (in some places they are actually called the Information Champion). Such an appointment will communicate the clear message that information management is a core aspect of the authority's functions.

Volume

The number of requests likely to be received each month should be calculated so that the level of commitment by the authority can be gauged. Experience of the amount of requests for information currently received will be important but the authority should bear in mind that there is likely to be a surge of requests in the early months of implementation. This may quieten down later in the year to a steady, consistent flow. Other factors that will have to be taken into account are:

- the profile of the organization (which might actually change as a result of interest generated by Freedom of Information requests); for example, the health sector may well be a major target for applicants
- events, planned or otherwise, directly affecting the authority
- level of advertising and marketing of the new legislation.

Resources

The authority must be prepared to commit resources to the project, especially in the early phase when interest from the public is likely to be high. A major commitment in the first year of implementation is likely to reap rewards and benefits for the organization in terms of its business efficiency and public profile, and serve it in good stead for the future.

2 Records management

Implementing Freedom of Information policies and procedures will be impossible without an effective records management system.

Advice and guidance on records management is enshrined in the Code of Practice under section 46 of the Act (see Chapter 6). Much help is also available from various websites, most notably:

- National Archives – www.nationalarchives.gov.uk
- Records Management Society – www.rms-gb.org.uk
- Joint Information Systems Committee – www.jisc.ac.uk.

The National Archives have also been instrumental in publishing model action plans for developing records management compliant with the Code of Practice. These are published on their website.

A vital part of ensuring that records are well managed in preparation for the implementation of FOI is knowing what information is held throughout the organization. It is more than likely that the extent of paper records and information is known but less likely that the same applies to electronic records and information. In general a good first step in making records management more effective is to undertake a records audit. This should include a survey of what information is held, how it is held, who created it, who uses it and how long it is required. Chapter 6 provides detailed guidance on undertaking an audit.

Part of examining the records management system might also include a consideration of the documents created. Are policy documents, minutes of meetings, etc. constructed in a FOI-friendly way? For example, will difficulties be caused by having to separate disclosable information from information that is subject to one or more exemptions?

The appointment of a records manager prior to and during the vital implementation phase of the Freedom of Information Act will go a long way towards ensuring that important accessibility and retrieval requirements are met. Although such a role may be separate for the first year or so, it might be combined with other information management responsibilities later.

3 Publication scheme

Make sure that the publication scheme can deliver what it promises and that the appropriate mechanisms are in place to make those deliveries. Consider also:

- staff awareness, in case they should receive enquiries about the scheme
- the scheme is available on a website, that links to other sites are still valid and effective
- whether mechanisms are in place for the regular release of information (for example, minutes of meetings, monthly reports, etc.)
- effectiveness of the complaints procedure.

4 Procedures for handling requests

Look at current enquiry procedures and see how these might be adapted to meet the requirements of the Code of Practice under section 45 of the Act (which sets out how public authorities should respond to requests for information). Establish the cost of dealing with enquiries so that estimates quoted in fees notices can be easily prepared.

Set up a tracking system so that requests can be monitored – not only to meet the 20-working-day deadline but also to record decisions so that any appeals can be dealt with effectively. Public authorities in the same sector may benefit from a linked tracking system, for example NHS Trusts, police authorities.

Consider the use of stock letters to deal with common enquiries, such as those which are referred to the website. Establish the complaints procedure and make sure that all those involved in it are aware of what is required. Make arrangements for these procedures to be published (as required by the section 45 Code of Practice).

5 Procedures for disclosure and exemption decisions

Ensure that other organizations with which the authority does business are aware of freedom of information and of any consequences that it may have for them. For example, the authority may hold information on behalf of third parties that may be subject to a FOI request. These parties will need to be aware of the time constraints under which the authority will operate and a suitable consultation phase may need to be incorporated within the deadline.

Appoint those people who will be responsible for making decisions on whether information can be released or withheld, and arrange for any necessary training.

Provide guidance on how to apply exemptions and make public interest decisions. This might include advice on when to consult other parties.

Consider the use of stock letters to deal with refusals (the Act requires certain information to be given to applicants in this instance).

Establish the complaints procedure and make sure that all those involved in it are aware of what is required. Make arrangements for these procedures to be published (as required by the section 45 Code of Practice).

6 Training

Basic awareness training on freedom of information should be included in induction programmes. Requests for information can be handed to any member of staff (or in the case of environmental requests, also by telephone) so they all need to be aware of what to do in that event. Consider also how familiarization of FOI might be imparted to existing staff – use of the intranet, newsletters, circulars and regular staff meetings.

Provide specialist training for those who will be dealing directly with freedom of information policies and procedures, such as those who will be making decisions on disclosure.

7 Publicity

Prepare clear and easy-to-understand guidance for the public, perhaps in the form of leaflets, so that they are well aware of how to make requests for information and of the type of service they will receive. Consider making available standard forms for applicants to request information. Publish on the website as well as in paper form.

8 Monitoring

Establish procedures and mechanisms for monitoring FOI implementation and requests for information. Set up systems for reporting and providing statistical information.

Tracking system

The benefits of having a system to log and track requests include:

- consistency in disclosure decisions
- effective handling of complaints and appeals
- management information (for example, frequently asked subjects, statistics, reports to the Information Commissioner)
- ability to redirect requests for information to the most relevant part of the organization (many members of the public will have only a vague idea of how government works and to which part of the organization requests should be sent)
- co-ordination of the release of information
- reduction in the duplication of information
- reduction in the costs of answering requests by minimizing appeals, letters to M.P.s, adverse press reports and staff time in handling applications.

There should be a central point in each public authority where requests will be directed and where the tracking system can be managed. Access to the tracking system should be provided to those who answer requests for information. A tracking system should be networked for particular groups of the public sector – such as NHS Trusts, government departments, faculties within a university and local authority departments. Such a networked system should have standard metadata to describe requests and standard fields to record outcomes. Some requests might cross these boundaries and public authorities may wish to consider wider access under special conditions.

A central tracking system will ensure that organizations are aware of requests which are relevant to their areas of interest, whether they are directed to them in the first instance or not, and will allow the co-ordination of decisions about releases of related material. Over time this may lead to the development of benchmarks for the release of information, thus speeding up the decision-making process and ensuring the consistency referred to above.

Once information has been released public authorities should also consider making available a description of it or the text itself over the internet, perhaps as a news item, or even including it within their publication scheme. Such action would certainly be within the spirit of the Act and would demonstrate greater openness. There is also, of course, the benefit of reduced individual requests when such action is undertaken. The tracking system itself may also be adapted for inclusion in the publication scheme.

Conclusion: a change in culture

Perhaps the most important aspect of preparing for the implementation of Freedom of Information – something that has to be borne in mind throughout – is the change of culture which the organization must inevitably undergo. This is something that needs to be managed carefully. It must come from the top of the organization and reach to its lowest point. See Figure 9.1.

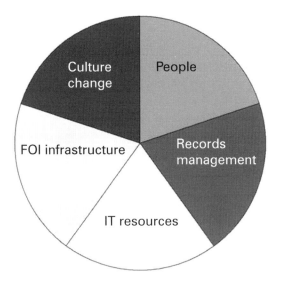

Figure 9.1   The essential elements of implementation

Signs of an organization fully prepared to meet the requirements of Freedom of Information

These are:

- consistent and standard record-keeping system across the organization
- ability to search and retrieve relevant information across the organization
- an effective publication scheme in place
- ability to deal with requests for information within 20 working days
- capability of providing information in preferred formats
- ability to provide information on and justifications of exemption decisions
- ability to deal with complaints
- all staff aware of Freedom of Information and good record-keeping practices
- assigned FOI staff with the expertise to advise and assist applicants
- attitude of staff at all levels moving towards a corporate and transparent culture.

Sample plan of a typical project

Project:	Freedom of Information	Project Manager:	
Project Sponsor:		Project Team:	
Last Amended:		Version:	

1 PROJECT BRIEF

1.1 Scope and background of the project

The commitment to legislate for freedom of information and to bring about more open government is part of the Government's programme of constitutional reform. The Freedom of Information Act 2000 enables members of the public to question decisions more closely and ensure that the services provided by the public sector are more efficiently and properly delivered.

The Act provides a right of access to recorded information held by public authorities, irrespective of the age of the information. It creates exemptions from the duty to disclose information and establishes the arrangements for enforcement and appeal. It also imposes duties on authorities with regard to the management of their records.

Ministers have decided that there will be no new money for implementing Freedom of Information. The increase in workload will need to be managed within existing resources. The [organization] will need to ensure that it manages its resources and puts in place sufficiently robust procedures to ensure that requests are dealt with within the time limit of 20 working days.

The project covers all of the [organization's] information in all formats including electronic.

1.2 Current position

The Freedom of Information Act received Royal Assent on 30 November 2000. The implementation timetable announced in November 2001 divides implementation into two phases as follows:

- Nov 2002 to June 2004 – publication schemes, approved by the Information Commissioner, must be in place
- Jan 2005 – the rights of access and associated provisions will be introduced.

A further factor affecting implementation is the issue of revised Environmental Information Regulations (EIR). The Regulations will govern access to environmental information irrespective of its date and are expected to be introduced in late 2003 (ahead of the FOI rights of access).

This means that between [2002/3] and January 2005 [*the organization*] must be equipped to provide information in accordance with its FOI publication scheme and respond to [*Openness Code requests*],[1] data subject access requests under the Data Protection Act 1998 and requests for environmental information under the EIR. This project takes account of these obligations.

1.3 Objectives
The principal objectives of the project are:

- Ensure that the records management system is efficient and effective enough to meet the requirements of FOI
- Staff of the organization are aware of FOI and suitable training is available
- A publication scheme is approved, made available and put into operation
- A system for handling requests for information, including disclosure/exemption decisions, is in place
- Establishment of an effective system for tracking FOI requests and disclosure decisions
- Provision of advice and guidance to the public.

1.4 The project aims to be completed by [*2004*].

1.5 Interfaces
The project will need to take account of the following projects and initiatives:

[*any current projects that may affect or impinge upon this project*]

2 DELIVERABLES
2.1 The final project plan will take the following form:

- Plan description (introduction, basis for the plan, plan structure)
- Quality plan (criteria and controls)
- Prerequisites and assumptions
- External dependencies
- Risk analysis
- Technical plan
- Resource plan
- Timetable.

2.2 The project will produce the following:

- Report
- FOI publication scheme
- Procedures for handling requests for information

- Drafting tracking system for managing requests and disclosure decisions
- Communications plan
- Training programme.

3 ASSUMPTIONS

The project assumes the following:

- That the requisite staff will be in place to enable implementation by January 2005
- The FOI tracking system can be implemented by January 2005.

4 INITIAL BUSINESS CASE

The [*organization*] is required to undertake this project as part of the implementation of the Freedom of Information Act 2000.

   The final report on the project will measure the benefits realized (or expected to be realized) by the implementation of the report in terms of:

- The management of [*the organization's*] records and information
- [*the organization's*] overall profile.

5 PROJECT ORGANIZATION STRUCTURE [2]

5.1 Project Board

The Project Board is responsible for ensuring delivery of implementation procedures and for signing off final procedures.

5.2 Individual members of the Project Board who represent particular business areas will contribute information and advice on the current use and handling of information in their areas, and how they can contribute to the implementation procedures.

5.3 The Project Manager reports to the Director of [*xxxxxxxxx*]. His/her responsibilities are:

- To manage the development and implementation of the overall project
- To ensure that the project is delivered on time
- To quality assure all documentation
- To prepare regular reports to the Director of [*xxxxxxxx*]
- To negotiate with the appropriate departments within [*the organization*] to procure the necessary resources for the project.

5.4 The Quality Assurance Co-ordinator . . .

5.5 The User Assurance Co-ordinator . . .

5.6 The Technical Assurance Co-ordinator . . .

6   QUALITY CONTROL

The quality of the project products will be assessed using the following criteria:

- Has the project been delivered on time and to cost?
- Has the project covered all parts of [*the organization*]?
- Have all staff in [*the organization*] been made aware of the project and been given the opportunity to comment or make suggestions?
- Do the proposals meet current statutory requirements, relevant codes of practice and relevant standards?
- Does the implementation plan meet the project specification?
- Does the implementation plan address the key issues?
- Are the products clear and easy to understand?
- Does the plan address the concerns and needs of all stakeholders?

7   CONTROLS

7.1 The Project Board will meet monthly to ensure that the project is on course to meet its objectives.

7.2 The Project Manager will ensure that the following documentation is maintained:

- Project initiation document
- Project Board minutes and papers
- Correspondence with Project Board members and project stakeholders
- Proposals and agreements for external work
- Monthly reports on progress
- Reports from external consultancy work.

7.3 The documentation will be available at all times to Project Board members and to the Director of [*xxxxxxxx*]. It will be kept until the end of the project at which time the Records Manager will appraise it for further retention. Normal rules of confidentiality will be observed.

8   EXCEPTION PROCESS

8.1 In the event of deviations from the plan the Project Manager will produce an exception report. This report will be agreed with the Project Board before being submitted to the Director of [*xxxxxxxx*].

8.2 On the basis of the exception report the Director of [*xxxxxxxx*], in consultation with the [*Chief Executive*], will authorise changes to the plan or different products from the project.

9   RISKS

Risk	Action	Responsibility

10   CONTINGENCY PLANS

11   PROJECT FILING STRUCTURE

11.1 The documentation outlined above will be maintained in a recognizable filing system. This will comprise four sections:

- Project documentation (PID, consultancy proposals, etc.)
- Reports
- Correspondence
- Project Board minutes and papers.

The files will be subject to normal review and disposal. The Records Manager will advise accordingly.

11.2 Electronic documents will be printed out and placed on files. They will also be kept on floppy disks by the Project Manager. Different versions of the same document will be numbered and dated.

Notes

1   Such as the Code of Practice on Access to Government Information or the Code of Practice on Openness in the NHS.

2   This will depend on the type of project that the organization adopts; that illustrated is allied to PRINCE methodology.

Appendix 1
Codes of Practice under sections 45 and 46 of the Freedom of Information Act 2000

Lord Chancellor's Code of Practice on the Discharge of Public Authorities' Functions under Part I of the Freedom of Information Act 2000, issued under section 45 of the Act (November 2002)

Foreword

Introduction

1. The Code of Practice, to which this is a foreword, fulfils the duty on the Lord Chancellor set out in section 45 of the Freedom of Information Act 2000, to provide guidance to public authorities as to the practice which it would, in his opinion, be desirable for them to follow in connection with the discharge of their functions under Part I of the Act. It is envisaged that Regulations to be made with respect to environmental information will make provision for the issue by the Secretary of State of a Code of Practice applying to the discharge of authorities' functions under those Regulations.

2. This foreword does not form part of the Code itself.

3. The Government is committed to greater openness in the public sector. The Freedom of Information Act will further this aim by helping to transform the culture of the public sector to one of greater openness, enabling members of the public to question the decisions of public authorities more closely and ensuring that services provided by the public sector are more efficiently and properly delivered. Conformity with the Code will assist this.

4. The Code is a supplement to the provisions in the Act. It is not a substitute for legislation. Public authorities should seek legal advice as considered nec-

essary on general issues relating to the implementation of the Act, or its application to individual cases.

Practice recommendations

5. Under the provisions of section 47 of the Act, the Information Commissioner has a duty to promote the observance of this Code by public authorities. If it appears to the Commissioner that the practice of a public authority in the exercise of its functions under Part I of the Act does not conform with that proposed in the Code of Practice, he may give to the authority a recommendation, under section 48 (known as a "practice recommendation"), specifying the steps which should, in his opinion, be taken to promote such conformity.

6. A practice recommendation must be given in writing and must refer to the particular provisions of the Code of Practice with which, in the Commissioner's opinion, the public authority's practice does not conform. A practice recommendation is simply a recommendation and cannot be directly enforced by the Information Commissioner. However, a failure to comply with a practice recommendation may lead to a failure to comply with the Act. Further, a failure to take account of a practice recommendation may lead to an adverse comment in a report to Parliament by the Commissioner.

7. It should be noted that because the provisions of the Act relating to the general right of access will not be brought into force until 1 January 2005, the Commissioner's powers to issue practice recommendations in relation to the handling of individual requests for information under the general right of access will not take effect before that date.

Information notices

8. The Information Commissioner determines whether the practice of a public authority conforms to the Code. Under section 51 of the Act, he may serve an information notice on the authority, requiring it to provide information relating to its conformity with the Code.

9. Under the provisions of section 54 of the Act, if a public authority fails to comply with an information notice, the Commissioner may certify in writing to the court that the public authority has failed to comply with that notice. The court may then inquire into the matter and, after hearing any witnesses who may be produced against or on behalf of, the public authority, and after hearing any statement that may be offered in defence, deal with the authority as if it had committed a contempt of court.

Duty to provide advice and assistance

10. Section 16 of the Act places a duty on public authorities to provide advice and assistance to applicants. A public authority is deemed to have complied with this duty in any particular case if it has conformed with the Code in relation to the provision of advice and assistance in that case. The duty to assist and advise is enforceable by the Information Commissioner. If a public authority fails in its statutory duty, the Commissioner may issue a decision notice under section 50, or an enforcement notice under section 52.

11. Public authorities should not forget that other Acts of Parliament may be relevant to the way in which authorities provide advice and assistance to applicants or potential applicants, e.g. the Disability Discrimination Act 1995 and the Race Relations Act 1976 (as amended by the Race Relations (Amendment) Act 2000).

Main features of the Act

12. The main features of the Freedom of Information Act 2000 are:
    i. a general right of access to recorded information held by public authorities, subject to certain conditions and exemptions;
    ii. in cases where information is exempted from disclosure, except where an absolute exemption applies, a duty on public authorities to:

    a. inform the applicant whether they hold the information requested, and
    b. communicate the information to him or her, unless the public interest in maintaining the exemption in question outweighs the public interest in disclosure;

    iii. a duty on every public authority to adopt and maintain a scheme, approved by the Commissioner, which relates to the publication of information by the authority, and to publish information in accordance with the scheme. An authority may adopt a model scheme approved by the Commissioner, which may have been prepared by the Commissioner or by other persons;
    iv. a new office of Information Commissioner with wide powers to enforce the rights created by the Act and to promote good practice, and a new Information Tribunal;
    v. a duty on the Lord Chancellor to promulgate Codes of Practice for guidance on specific issues.

Copyright

13. Public authorities should be aware that information which is disclosed under the Act may be subject to copyright protection. If an applicant wishes to use

any such information in a way that would infringe copyright, for example by making multiple copies, or issuing copies to the public, he or she would require a licence from the copyright holder. HMSO have issued guidance on this subject in relation to Crown Copyright, which is available on HMSO's website at (http://www.hmso.gov.uk/g-note19.htm) or by contacting HMSO at: HMSO Licensing Division, St Clements House, 2-16 Colegate, Norwich NR3 1BQ; Tel: 01613-621000, Fax: 01603-723000, e-mail: HMSO Licensing.

Training

14. All communications in writing to a public authority, including those transmitted by electronic means, potentially amount to a request for information within the meaning of the Act, and if they do, they must be dealt with in accordance with the provisions of the Act. It is therefore essential that everyone working in a public authority who deals with correspondence, or who otherwise may be required to provide information, is familiar with the requirements of the Act and the Codes of Practice issued under its provisions and takes account of any relevant guidance on good practice issued by the Commissioner. Authorities should ensure that proper training is provided in this regard.

15. In planning and delivering training authorities should be aware of other provisions affecting the disclosure of information such as Environmental Information Regulations and the Data Protection Act 1998.

CODE OF PRACTICE
On the Discharge of the Functions of Public Authorities under Part I of the Freedom of Information Act 2000

The Lord Chancellor, after consulting the Information Commissioner, issues the following Code of Practice pursuant to section 45 of the Act.

Laid before Parliament on 20 November 2002 pursuant to section 45(5) of the Freedom of Information Act 2000.

I   Introduction

1. This code of practice outlines to public authorities the practice which it would, in the opinion of the Lord Chancellor, be desirable for them to follow in connection with the discharge of their functions under Part I (Access to information held by public authorities) of the Freedom of Information Act 2000 ("the Act").

2. The aims of the Code are to:

- facilitate the disclosure of information under the Act by setting out good administrative practice that it is desirable for public authorities to follow when handling requests for information, including, where appropriate, the transfer of a request to a different authority;
- protect the interests of applicants by setting out standards for the provision of advice which it would be good practice to make available to them and to encourage the development of effective means of complaining about decisions taken under the Act;
- ensure that the interests of third parties who may be affected by any decision to disclose information are considered by the authority by setting standards for consultation; and
- ensure that authorities consider the implications for Freedom of Information before agreeing to confidentiality provisions in contracts and accepting information in confidence from a third party more generally.

3.   Although there is a statutory duty on the Lord Chancellor to issue the Code, the provisions of the Code themselves do not have statutory force. However, authorities are expected to abide by the Code unless there are good reasons, capable of being justified to the Information Commissioner, why it would be inappropriate to do so. The statutory requirements for dealing with requests for information are contained in the Act and regulations made under it and public authorities must comply with these statutory provisions at all times. However, section 47 of the Act places a duty on the Information Commissioner to promote the following of good practice by public authorities ("good practice" includes compliance with the provisions of the Code), and section 48 of the Act enables the Information Commissioner to issue a "practice recommendation" to a public authority if it appears to him that the practice of the authority does not conform with that proposed in the Code. Further, section 16 of the Act places a duty on public authorities to provide advice and assistance to applicants and potential applicants. Authorities will have complied with this duty in any particular case if they have conformed with the Code in relation to the provision of advice or assistance in that case.

4.   Words and expressions used in this Code have the same meaning as the same words and expressions used in the Act.

II   The provision of advice and assistance to persons making requests for information

5.   Every public authority should be ready to provide advice and assistance, including but not necessarily limited to the steps set out below, to those who propose to make, or have made requests to it, in order to facilitate their use of the Act. The duty on the public authority is to provide advice and assistance "so far as it would be reasonable to expect the authority to do so". Any pub-

lic authority which conforms with this Code in relation to the provision of advice and assistance in any case will be taken to comply with this duty in relation to that case.

6. Public authorities should publish their procedures for dealing with requests for information. These procedures may include what the public authority's usual procedure will be where it does not hold the information requested. (See also VI – "Transferring requests for information".) It may also alert potential applicants to the fact that the public authority may need to consult other public authorities and/or third parties in order to reach a decision on whether the requested information can be released, and therefore alert potential applicants that they may wish to be notified before any transfer of request or consultation is made and if so, they should say so in their applications. (See also VII – "Consultation with third parties".) The procedures should include an address or addresses (including an e-mail address where possible) to which applicants may direct requests for information or for assistance. A telephone number should also be provided, where possible that of a named individual who can provide assistance. These procedures should be referred to in the authority's publication scheme.

7. Staff working in public authorities in contact with the public should bear in mind that not everyone will be aware of the Act, or Regulations made under it, and they will need to draw these to the attention of potential applicants who appear unaware of them.

8. A request for information under the Act's general right of access must be made in writing (which includes a request transmitted by electronic means which is received in legible form and is capable of being used for subsequent reference). Where a person is unable to frame their request in writing, the public authority should ensure that appropriate assistance is given to enable that person to make a request for information. Depending on the circumstances, appropriate assistance might include:

- advising the person that another person or agency (such as a Citizens Advice Bureau) may be able to assist them with the application, or make the application on their behalf;
- in exceptional circumstances, offering to take a note of the application over the telephone and then send the note to the applicant for confirmation (in which case the written note of the telephone request, once verified by the applicant and returned, would constitute a written request for information and the statutory time limit for reply would begin when the written confirmation was received).

This list is not exhaustive, and public authorities should be flexible in offering advice and assistance most appropriate to the circumstances of the applicant.

9. Where the applicant does not describe the information sought in a way which would enable the public authority to identify or locate it, or the request is ambiguous, the authority should, as far as practicable, provide assistance to the applicant to enable him or her to describe more clearly the information requested. Authorities should be aware that the aim of providing assistance is to clarify the nature of the information sought, not to determine the aims or motivation of the applicant. Care should be taken not to give the applicant the impression that he or she is obliged to disclose the nature of his or her interest or that he or she will be treated differently if he or she does. It is important that the applicant is contacted as soon as possible, preferably by telephone, fax or e-mail, where more information is needed to clarify what is sought.

10. Appropriate assistance in this instance might include:

- providing an outline of the different kinds of information which might meet the terms of the request;
- providing access to detailed catalogues and indexes, where these are available, to help the applicant ascertain the nature and extent of the information held by the authority;
- providing a general response to the request setting out options for further information which could be provided on request.

This list is not exhaustive, and public authorities should be flexible in offering advice and assistance most appropriate to the circumstances of the applicant.

11. In seeking to clarify what is sought public authorities should bear in mind that applicants cannot reasonably be expected to possess identifiers such as a file reference number, or a description of a particular record, unless this information is made available by the authority for the use of applicants.

12. If, following the provision of such assistance, the applicant still fails to describe the information requested in a way which would enable the authority to identify and locate it, the authority is not expected to seek further clarification. The authority should disclose any information relating to the application which has been successfully identified and found for which it does not wish to claim an exemption. It should also explain to the applicant why it cannot take the request any further and provide details of the authority's complaints procedure and the applicant's rights under section 50 of the Act (see "Complaints procedure" in section XII below).

13. Where the applicant indicates that he or she is not prepared to pay the fee notified in any fees notice given to the applicant, the authority should consider whether there is any information that may be of interest to the applicant that is available free of charge.

14. Where an authority is not obliged to comply with a request for information because, under section 12(1) and regulations made under section 12(4), the

cost of complying would exceed the "appropriate limit" (i.e. cost threshold), and where the public authority is not prepared to comply on a discretionary basis because of the cost of doing so, the authority should consider providing an indication of what information could be provided within the cost ceiling.

15. An authority is not expected to provide assistance to applicants whose requests are vexatious within the meaning of section 14 of the Act.

III   Handling requests for information which appear to be part of an organised campaign

16. Where an authority is not required to comply with a number of related requests because, under section 12(1) and regulations made under section 12(4), the cumulative cost of complying with the requests would exceed the "appropriate limit" (i.e. cost threshold) prescribed in Fees Regulations, the authority should consider whether the information could be disclosed in another, more cost-effective, manner. For example, the authority should consider if the information is such that publication on the authority's website, and a brief notification of the website reference to each applicant, would bring the cost within the appropriate limit.

IV   Timeliness in dealing with requests for information

17. Public authorities are required to comply with all requests for information promptly and they should not delay responding until the end of the 20 working day period under section 10(1) if the information could reasonably have been provided earlier.

18. Public authorities should aim to make *all* decisions within 20 working days, including in cases where a public authority needs to consider where the public interest lies in respect of an application for exempt information. However, it is recognised there will be some instances where it will not be possible to deal with such an application within 20 working days. Although there is no statutory time limit on the length of time the authority may take to reach a decision where the public interest must be considered, it must, under section 17(2), give an estimate of the date by which it expects to reach such a decision. In these instances, authorities are expected to give estimates which are realistic and reasonable in the circumstances of the particular case, taking account, for example, of the need to consult third parties where this is necessary. Public authorities are expected to comply with their estimates unless there are good reasons not to. If the public authority exceeds its estimate, it should apologise to the applicant and explain the reason(s) for the delay. If a public authority finds, while considering the public interest, that the estimate given is proving unrealistic, it should keep the applicant informed. Public authorities should keep a record of instances where estimates are exceeded,

and where this happens more than occasionally, take steps to identify the problem and rectify it.

V   Charging fees

19. The Act does not require charges to be made, but public authorities have discretion to charge applicants a fee in accordance with Fees Regulations made under sections 9, 12 and 13 of the Act in respect of requests made under the general right of access.

20. The Fees Regulations do not apply:

- to material made available under a publication scheme under section 19;
- to information which is reasonably accessible to the applicant by other means within the meaning of the exemption provided for at section 21; or
- where provision is made by or under any enactment as to the fee that may be charged by the public authority for disclosure of the information as provided in sections 9(5) and 13(3) of the Act.

Public authorities should ensure that any charges they make in cases falling outside those covered by the Fees Regulations are in accordance with any relevant legislation and are within the terms of any relevant guidance which has been issued or approved by HM Treasury and which is applicable to the public authority, or any relevant guidance issued or approved by the Northern Ireland Department of Finance and Personnel applicable to devolved public bodies in Northern Ireland.

VI   Transferring requests for information

21. A request can only be transferred where a public authority receives a request for information which it does not hold, within the meaning of section 3(2) of the Act, but which is held by another public authority. If a public authority in receipt of a request holds some of the information requested, a transfer can only be made in respect of the information it does not hold (but is held by another public authority).

22. Public authorities should bear in mind that ''holding'' information includes holding a copy of a record produced or supplied by another person or body (but does not extend to holding a record on behalf of another person or body as provided for in section 3(2)(a) of the Act).

23. The authority receiving the initial request must always process it in accordance with the Act in respect of such information relating to the request as it holds. The authority should also advise the applicant that it does not hold part of the requested information, or all of it, whichever applies. But before doing this,

the authority must be certain as to the extent of the information relating to the request which it holds itself.

24. If the authority to whom the original request was made believes that some or all of the information requested is held by another public authority, the authority should consider what would be the most helpful way of assisting the applicant with his or her request. In most cases this is likely to involve:

  • contacting the applicant and informing him or her that the information requested may be held by another public authority;
  • suggesting that the applicant re-applies to the authority which the original authority believes to hold the information;
  • providing him or her with contact details for that authority.

25. However, in some cases the authority to whom the original request is made may consider it to be more appropriate to transfer the request to another authority in respect of the information which it does not hold. In such cases, the authority should consult the other authority with a view to ascertaining whether it does hold the information and, if so, consider whether it should transfer the request to it. A request (or part of a request) should not be transferred without confirmation by the second authority that it holds the information.

26. Before transferring a request for information to another authority, the authority should consider:

  • whether a transfer is appropriate; and if so
  • whether the applicant is likely to have any grounds to object to the transfer.

If the authority reasonably concludes that the applicant is not likely to object, it may transfer the request without going back to the applicant, but should tell him or her it has done so.

27. Where there are reasonable grounds to believe an applicant is likely to object, the authority should only transfer the request to another authority with his or her consent. If the authority is in any doubt, it may prefer to contact the applicant with a view to suggesting that he or she makes a new request to the other authority, as in paragraph 23 above.

28. Where a request or part of a request is transferred from one public authority to another, the receiving authority must comply with its obligations under Part I of the Act in the same way as it would for a request that is received direct from an applicant. The time for complying with such a request will be measured from the day that the receiving authority receives the request.

29. All transfers of requests should take place as soon as is practicable, and the applicant should be informed as soon as possible once this has been done.

30. Where a public authority is unable either to advise the applicant which public authority holds, or may hold, the requested information or to facilitate the transfer of the request to another authority (or considers it inappropriate to do so) it should consider what advice, if any, it can provide to the applicant to enable him or her to pursue his or her request.

VII   Consultation with third parties

31. In some cases the disclosure of information pursuant to a request may affect the legal rights of a third party, for example where information is subject to the common law duty of confidence or where it constitutes "personal data" within the meaning of the Data Protection Act 1998 ("the DPA"). Public authorities must always remember that unless an exemption provided for in the Act applies in relation to any particular information, they will be obliged to disclose that information in response to a request.

32. Where a disclosure of information cannot be made without the consent of a third party (for example, where information has been obtained from a third party and in the circumstances the disclosure of the information without their consent would constitute an actionable breach of confidence such that the exemption at section 41 of the Act would apply), the authority should consult that third party with a view to seeking their consent to the disclosure, unless such a consultation is not practicable, for example because the third party cannot be located or because the costs of consulting them would be disproportionate.

33. Where information constitutes "personal data" within the meaning of the DPA, public authorities should have regard to section 40 of the Act which makes detailed provision for cases in which a request relates to such information and the interplay between the Act and the DPA in such cases.

34. Where the interests of the third party which may be affected by a disclosure do not give rise to legal rights, consultation may still be appropriate.

35. Consultation should take place where:

- the views of the third party may assist the authority to determine whether an exemption under the Act applies to the information requested; or
- the views of the third party may assist the authority to determine where the public interest lies under section 2 of the Act.

36. A public authority may consider that consultation is not appropriate where the cost of consulting with third parties would be disproportionate. In such cases, the authority should consider what is the most reasonable course of action for it to take in light of the requirements of the Act and the individual circumstances of the request.

37. Consultation will be unnecessary where:

- the public authority does not intend to disclose the information relying on some other legitimate ground under the terms of the Act;
- the views of the third party can have no effect on the decision of the authority, for example, where there is other legislation preventing or requiring the disclosure of this information;
- no exemption applies and so under the Act's provisions, the information must be provided.

38. Where the interests of a number of third parties may be affected by a disclosure and those parties have a representative organisation which can express views on behalf of those parties, the authority may, if it considers consultation appropriate, consider that it would be sufficient to consult that representative organisation. If there is no representative organisation, the authority may consider that it would be sufficient to consult a representative sample of the third parties in question.

39. The fact that the third party has not responded to consultation does not relieve the authority of its duty to disclose information under the Act, or its duty to reply within the time specified in the Act.

40. In all cases, it is for the public authority, not the third party (or representative of the third party) to determine whether or not information should be disclosed under the Act. A refusal to consent to disclosure by a third party does not, in itself, mean information should be withheld.

VIII   Freedom of Information and public sector contracts

41. When entering into contracts public authorities should refuse to include contractual terms which purport to restrict the disclosure of information held by the authority and relating to the contract beyond the restrictions permitted by the Act. Public authorities cannot "contract out" of their obligations under the Act. Unless an exemption provided for under the Act is applicable in relation to any particular information, a public authority will be obliged to disclose that information in response to a request, regardless of the terms of any contract.

42. When entering into contracts with non-public authority contractors, public authorities may be under pressure to accept confidentiality clauses so that information relating to the terms of the contract, its value and performance will be exempt from disclosure. Public authorities should reject such clauses wherever possible. Where, exceptionally, it is necessary to include non-disclosure provisions in a contract, an option could be to agree with the contractor a schedule of the contract which clearly identifies information which should not be disclosed. But authorities will need to take care when drawing up any such schedule, and be aware that any restrictions on disclosure provided for could

potentially be overridden by their obligations under the Act, as described in the paragraph above.

43. In any event, public authorities should not agree to hold information 'in confidence' which is not in fact confidential in nature. Authorities should be aware that the exemption provided for in section 41 only applies if information has been obtained by a public authority from another person, and the disclosure of the information to the public, otherwise than under the Act, would constitute a breach of confidence actionable by that, or any other person.

44. Any acceptance of such confidentiality provisions must be for good reasons and capable of being justified to the Commissioner.

45. It is for the public authority to disclose information pursuant to the Act, and not the non-public authority contractor. However, the public authority may wish to protect from disclosure by the contractor, by appropriate contractual terms, information which the authority has provided to the contractor which would clearly be exempt from disclosure under the Act, by appropriate contractual terms. In order to avoid unnecessary secrecy, any such constraints should be drawn as narrowly as possible, and according to the individual circumstances of the case. Apart from such cases, public authorities should not impose terms of secrecy on contractors.

46. Section 5(1)(b) of the Act empowers the Lord Chancellor to designate as public authorities for the purposes of the Act, persons (or bodies) who provide under a contract made with a public authority, any service whose provision is a function of that authority. Thus, some non-public authority contractors will be regarded as public authorities within the meaning of the Act, although only in respect of the services provided under the contract. As such, and to that extent, the contractor will be required to comply with the Act like any other public authority.

IX   Accepting information in confidence from third parties

47. A public authority should only accept information from third parties in confidence if it is necessary to obtain that information in connection with the exercise of any of the authority's functions and it would not otherwise be provided. In addition, public authorities should not agree to hold information received from third parties "in confidence" which is not confidential in nature. Again, acceptance of any confidentiality provisions must be for good reasons, capable of being justified to the Commissioner.

X   Consultation with devolved administrations

48. Public authorities should consult with the relevant devolved administration before disclosing information provided by or directly concerning that administration, except where:

- the views of the devolved administration can have no effect on the decision of the authority (for example where there is other legislation requiring the disclosure of the information), or there is no applicable exemption so the information must be disclosed under the Act; or
- in the circumstances, consultation would be disproportionate.

49. Similarly, the devolved administrations should consult with the relevant non-devolved public authority before disclosing information provided by or directly concerning that authority, except where the views of the public authority can have no effect on the decision whether to disclose, or where consultation would be disproportionate in the circumstances.

XI   Refusal of request

50. Where a request for information is refused in reliance on an exemption, the Act requires that the authority notifies the applicant which exemption has been claimed, and if it would otherwise not be apparent, why that exemption applies. Public authorities should not (subject to the proviso in section 17(4) i.e. if the statement would involve the disclosure of information which would itself be exempt information) merely paraphrase the wording of the exemption. The Act also requires authorities, when withholding information (other than under an "absolute" exemption), to state the reasons for claiming that the public interest in maintaining the exemption outweighs the public interest in disclosure. Public authorities should specify the public interest factors (for and against disclosure) which they have taken into account before reaching the decision (again, subject to the proviso in section 17(4)).

51. For monitoring purposes public authorities should keep a record of all applications where either all or part of the requested information is withheld. In addition to a record of the numbers of applications involved where information is withheld, senior managers in each public authority need information on each case to determine whether cases are being properly considered, and whether the reasons for refusals are sound. This could be done by requiring all staff who refuse a request for information to forward the details to a central point in the organization for collation. Details of information on complaints about applications which have been refused (see XII – "Complaints procedure" below) could be collected at the same central point.

XII   Complaints procedure

52. Each public authority should have a complaints procedure in place by the date that its duties in respect of the publication scheme provisions of the Act come into effect. The complaints procedure may then be used by any person who perceives that the authority is not complying with its publication scheme. If the matter cannot be dealt with satisfactorily on an informal basis, the pub-

lic authority should inform such persons if approached by them of the details of its internal complaints procedure, and how to contact the Information Commissioner, if the complainant wishes to write to him about the matter. The authority should also explain that although the complainant cannot apply to the Commissioner for a decision under section 50 of the Act, the Commissioner may investigate the matter at his discretion.

53. When the provisions of the Act relating to the general right of access come into force, the complaints procedure will also be required for dealing with complaints from people who consider that their request has not been properly handled, or who are otherwise dissatisfied with the outcome of the consideration of their request, and where the issue is such that it cannot be resolved informally in discussion with the official dealing with the request. If a public authority has failed to introduce a complaints procedure, an applicant is entitled, under the Act, to complain directly to the Commissioner.

54. When communicating any decision made in relation to a request under the Act's general right of access, public authorities are obliged, under section 17(7) of the Act, to notify the applicant of their rights of complaint. They should provide details of their own complaints procedure, including how to make a complaint and inform the applicant of the right to complain to the Commissioner under section 50 if he or she is still dissatisfied following the authority's review.

55. Any written reply from the applicant (including one transmitted by electronic means) expressing dissatisfaction with an authority's response to a valid request for information should be treated as a complaint, as should any written communication from a person who perceives the authority is not complying with its publication scheme. These communications should be handled in accordance with the authority's complaints procedure, even if, in the case of a request for information under the general right of access, the applicant does not state his or her desire for the authority to review their decision or their handling of the application.

56. The complaints procedure should be a fair and impartial means of dealing with handling problems and reviewing decisions taken pursuant to the Act, including decisions taken about where the public interest lies in respect of exempt information. It should be possible to reverse or otherwise amend decisions previously taken. Complaints procedures should be clear and not unnecessarily bureaucratic. They should be capable of producing a prompt determination of the complaint.

57. Where the complaint concerns a request for information under the general right of access, the review should be handled by a person who was not a party to the original decision, where this is practicable. If this is not possible (for example in a very small public authority), the circumstances should be explained to the applicant. Where the decision on the application was taken by someone in a position where a review cannot realistically be undertaken (e.g.

a Minister), the public authority may consider whether to waive the internal review procedure (and inform the applicant if this is what is decided), so that the applicant is free to approach the Commissioner.

58. In all cases, complaints should be acknowledged and the complainant should be informed of the authority's target date for determining the complaint. Where it is apparent that determination of the complaint will take longer than the target time (for example because of the complexity of the particular case), the authority should inform the applicant and explain the reason for the delay. The complainant should always be informed of the outcome of his or her complaint.

59. Authorities may set their own target times for dealing with complaints but these should be reasonable, defensible, and subject to regular review. Each public authority should publish its target times for determining complaints and information as to how successful it is with meeting those targets.

60. Records should be kept of all complaints and of their outcome. Authorities should have procedures in place for monitoring complaints and for reviewing, and, if necessary, amending, procedures for dealing with requests for information where such action is indicated by more than occasional reversals of initial decisions.

61. Where the outcome of a complaint is that information should be disclosed which was previously withheld, the information in question should be disclosed as soon as practicable and the applicant should be informed how soon this will be.

62. Where the outcome of a complaint is that the procedures within an authority have not been properly followed by the authority's staff, the authority should apologise to the applicant. The authority should also take appropriate steps to prevent similar errors occurring in future.

63. Where the outcome of a complaint is that an initial decision to withhold information is upheld, or is otherwise in the authority's favour, the applicant should be informed of his or her right to apply to the Commissioner, and be given details of how to make an application, for a decision on whether the request for information has been dealt with in accordance with the requirements of Part I of the Act.

Lord Chancellor's Code of Practice on the Management of Records, issued under section 46 of the Freedom of Information Act 2000 (November 2002)[1]

FOREWORD

General

(i)   This Code of Practice (hereafter referred to as 'the Code') provides guidance to all public authorities as to the practice which it would, in the opinion of the Lord Chancellor, be desirable for them to follow in connection with the discharge of their functions under the Freedom of Information Act 2000 (FOIA). The Code applies also to other bodies that are subject to the Public Records Act 1958 and the Public Records Act (NI) 1923.

(ii)   The Code fulfils the duty of the Lord Chancellor under section 46 of the FOIA.

(iii)   Any freedom of information legislation is only as good as the quality of the records to which it provides access. Such rights are of little use if reliable records are not created in the first place, if they cannot be found when needed or if the arrangements for their eventual archiving or destruction are inadequate. Consequently, all public authorities are strongly encouraged to pay heed to the guidance in the Code.

(iv)   The Code is a supplement to the provisions in the FOIA. But its adoption will help authorities to comply with their duties under that Act. It is not a substitute for legislation. Public authorities should seek legal advice as appropriate on general issues relating to the implementation of the FOIA, or its application to individual cases. The Code is complemented by the Code of Practice under section 45 of the FOIA and by Memoranda of Understanding setting out how the consultation requirements of section 66 of the FOIA will be put into effect.

(v)   The Information Commissioner will promote the observance of the Code by public authorities, acting as required by the FOIA. If it appears to the Commissioner that the practice of an authority in relation to the exercise of its functions under the FOIA does not conform with that set out in the Code, he may issue a practice recommendation under section 48 of the Act. A practice recommendation must be in writing and must specify the provisions of the Code which have not been met and the steps which should, in his opinion, be taken to promote conformity with Code.

(vi)   If the Commissioner reasonably requires any information for the purpose of determining whether the practice of a public authority in relation to the exercise of its functions under the FOIA conforms with that proposed in this Code, he may serve on the authority a notice (known as an 'information notice') under the provisions of section 51 of the Act. This requires it, within such time as is specified in the notice, to furnish the Commissioner, in such form as may be so specified, with such information relating to conformity with the Code of Practice as is so specified.

(vii)   An information notice must contain a statement that the Commissioner regards the specified information as relevant for the purpose of deciding whether the practice of the authority conforms with that proposed in the Code of Practice and of his reasons for regarding that information as relevant for that purpose. It must also contain particulars of the rights of appeal conferred by section 57 of the FOIA.

(viii) Authorities should note that if they are failing to comply with the Code, they may also be failing to comply with the Public Records Acts 1958 and 1967, the Local Government (Records) Act 1962, the Local Government Act 1972, the Local Government (Access to Information) Act 1985 or other record-keeping or archives legislation, and they may consequently be in breach of their statutory obligations.

(ix) The Public Records Act (NI) 1923 sets out the duties of public record bodies in Northern Ireland in respect of the records they create and requires that records should be transferred to, and preserved by, the Public Record Office of Northern Ireland.

Main features of the FOIA

(x) The main features of the FOIA are:

1. a general right of access to recorded information held by a wide range of bodies across the public sector, subject to certain conditions and exemptions. The right includes provisions in respect of historical records which are more than 30 years old.

2. in relation to most exempt information, the information must nonetheless be disclosed unless the public interest in maintaining the exemption in question outweighs the public interest in disclosure.

3. a duty on every public authority to adopt and maintain a scheme which relates to the publication of information by the authority and is approved by the Information Commissioner. Authorities must publish information in accordance with their publication schemes. This scheme must specify:

   • classes of information which the public authority publishes or intends to publish;
   • the manner in which information of each class is, or is intended to be, published; and
   • whether the material is, or is intended to be, available to the public free of charge, or on payment.

4. a new office of Information Commissioner and a new Information Tribunal, with wide powers to enforce the rights created and to promote good practice;

5. a duty on the Lord Chancellor to promulgate Codes of Practice for guidance on specific issues;

6. the amendment of the public records system to integrate it with the new right of access under the FOIA.

Training

(xi)   All communications in writing (including by electronic means) to a public authority fall within the scope of the FOIA, if they seek information, and must be dealt with in accordance with the provisions of the Act. It is therefore essential that everyone working in a public authority is familiar with the provisions of the FOIA, the Codes of Practice issued under its provisions, any relevant Memoranda of Understanding, and any relevant guidance on good practice issued by the Commissioner. Authorities should ensure that proper training is provided.

(xii) In planning and delivering training, authorities should be aware of other provisions affecting the disclosure of information, such as the Environmental Information Regulations 1992 and their successors which, for example, do not require requests to be in writing.

Authorities subject to the Public Records Acts

(xiii) The guidance on records management and on the transfer of public records in the Code should be read in the context of existing legislation on record-keeping. In particular, the Public Records Act 1958 (as amended) gives duties to public record bodies in respect of the records they create. It also requires the Keeper of Public Records to supervise the discharge of those duties. Authorities that are subject to the Public Records Acts 1958 and 1967 should note that if they are failing to comply with the Code, they may also be failing to comply with those Acts.

(xiv) The Public Records Act (NI) 1923 sets out the duties of public record bodies in Northern Ireland in respect of the records they create and requires that records should be transferred to, and preserved by, the Public Record Office of Northern Ireland.

(xv)   The Information Commissioner will promote the observance of the Code in consultation with the Keeper of Public Records when dealing with bodies which are subject to the Public Records Acts 1958 and 1967 and with the Deputy Keeper of the Records of Northern Ireland for bodies subject to the Public Records Act (NI) 1923.

(xvi) If it appears to the Commissioner that the practice of an authority in relation to the exercise of its functions under the FOIA does not conform with that set out in the Code, he may issue a practice recommendation under Section 48 of the Act. Before issuing such a recommendation to a body subject to the Public Records Acts 1958 and 1967 or the Public Records Act (NI) 1923, the Commissioner shall consult the Keeper of Public Records or the Deputy Keeper of the Records of Northern Ireland.

(xvii) The content of this Code has been agreed by the Deputy Keeper of Records of Northern Ireland. Part Two, in particular, describes the roles which public record bodies should perform to ensure the timely and effective review and transfer of public records to the Public Record Office or to places of deposit (as defined in Section 4 of the Public Records Act 1958) or to the Public Record Office of Northern Ireland (under the Public Records Act 1958 or the Public Records Act (NI) 1923). For the avoidance of doubt the term 'public records' includes Welsh public records as defined by Sections 116-118 of the Government of Wales Act 1998.

Role of the Lord Chancellor's Advisory Council on Public Records and of the Public Record Office

(xviii) To advise authorities on the review of public records, the Lord Chancellor, having received the advice of his Advisory Council on Public Records, (hereafter 'the Advisory Council') may prepare and issue guidance. This may include advice on the periods of time for which the Advisory Council considers it appropriate to withhold categories of sensitive records beyond the 30 year period. In Northern Ireland similar guidance shall be issued by the Deputy Keeper of the Records of Northern Ireland following consultation with the Departments responsible for the records affected by the guidance.

(xix) The Public Record Office will provide support as appropriate to the Advisory Council in its consideration of applications from authorities in respect of public records and in its preparation of guidance to authorities. In Northern Ireland the Public Record Office of Northern Ireland will provide similar support to the Sensitivity Review Group.

CODE OF PRACTICE

On (1) the management of records by public authorities and (2) the transfer and review of public records under the Freedom of Information Act 2000

The Lord Chancellor, after consulting the Information Commissioner and the appropriate Northern Ireland Minister, issues the following Code of Practice pursuant to section 46 of the Freedom of Information Act.

Laid before Parliament on 20 November 2002 pursuant to section 46(6) of the Freedom of Information Act 2000.

INTRODUCTION

1   *The aims of the Code are:*

(1) to set out practices which public authorities, and bodies subject to the Public Records Act 1958 and the Public Records Act (NI) 1923,

should follow in relation to the creation, keeping, management and destruction of their records (Part One of the Code), and

(2) to describe the arrangements which public record bodies should follow in reviewing public records and transferring them to the Public Record Office or to places of deposit or to the Public Record Office of Northern Ireland (Part Two of the Code).

2   This Code refers to records in all technical or physical formats.

3   Part One of the Code provides a framework for the management of records of public authorities and of bodies subject to the Public Records Act 1958 and the Public Records Act (NI) 1923, and Part Two deals with the review and transfer of public records. More detailed guidance on both themes may be obtained from published standards.

4   Words and expressions used in this Code have the same meaning as the same words and expressions used in the FOIA.

PART ONE: RECORDS MANAGEMENT

5   *Functional Responsibility*

5.1   The records management function should be recognised as a specific corporate programme within an authority and should receive the necessary levels of organizational support to ensure effectiveness. It should bring together responsibilities for records in all formats, including electronic records, throughout their life cycle, from planning and creation through to ultimate disposal. It should have clearly defined responsibilities and objectives, and the resources to achieve them. It is desirable that the person, or persons, responsible for the records management function should also have either direct responsibility or an organisational connection with the person or persons responsible for freedom of information, data protection and other information management issues.

6   *Policy*

6.1   An authority should have in place an overall policy statement, endorsed by top management and made readily available to staff at all levels of the organisation, on how it manages its records, including electronic records.

6.2   This policy statement should provide a mandate for the performance of all records and information management functions. In particular, it should set out an authority's commitment to create, keep and manage records which document its principal activities. The policy should also outline the role of records management and its relationship to the authority's overall strategy; define roles and responsibilities including the responsibility of individuals to document their actions and decisions in the authority's records, and to dispose of records; provide a framework for supporting standards, procedures and guidelines; and indicate the way in which compliance with the policy and its supporting standards, procedures and guidelines will be monitored.

6.3   The policy statement should be reviewed at regular intervals (at least once every three years) and, if appropriate, amended to maintain its relevance.

7   Human Resources

7.1   A designated member of staff of appropriate seniority should have lead responsibility for records management within the authority. This lead role should be formally acknowledged and made known throughout the authority.

7.2   Staff responsible for records management should have the appropriate skills and knowledge needed to achieve the aims of the records management programme. Responsibility for all aspects of record keeping should be specifically defined and incorporated in the role descriptions or similar documents.

7.3   Human resource policies and practices in organisations should address the need to recruit and retain good quality staff and should accordingly support the records management function in the following areas:

- the provision of appropriate resources to enable the records management function to be maintained across all of its activities;
- the establishment and maintenance of a scheme, such as a competency framework, to identify the knowledge, skills and corporate competencies required in records and information management;
- the regular review of selection criteria for posts with records management duties to ensure currency and compliance with best practice;
- the regular analysis of training needs;
- the establishment of a professional development programme for staff with records management duties;
- the inclusion in induction training programmes for all new staff of an awareness of records issues and practices.

8   Active Records Management

Record Creation

8.1   Each operational/business unit of an authority should have in place an adequate system for documenting its activities. This system should take into account the legislative and regulatory environments in which the authority works.

8.2   Records of a business activity should be complete and accurate enough to allow employees and their successors to undertake appropriate actions in the context of their responsibilities, to

- facilitate an audit or examination of the business by anyone so authorised,
- protect the legal and other rights of the authority, its clients and any other person affected by its actions, and
- provide authenticity of the records so that the evidence derived from them is shown to be credible and authoritative.

8.3   Records created by the authority should be arranged in a record keeping system that will enable the authority to obtain the maximum benefit from the quick and easy retrieval of information.

Record Keeping

8.4   Installing and maintaining an effective records management programme depends on knowledge of what records are held, in what form they are made accessible, and their relationship to organisational functions. An information survey or record audit will meet this requirement, help to promote control over the records, and provide valuable data for developing records appraisal and disposal procedures.

8.5   Paper and electronic record-keeping systems should contain metadata (descriptive and technical documentation) to enable the system and the records to be understood and to be operated efficiently, and to provide an administrative context for effective management of the records.

8.6   The record-keeping system, whether paper or electronic, should include a set of rules for referencing, titling, indexing and, if appropriate, security marking of records. These should be easily understood and should enable the efficient retrieval of information.

Record Maintenance

8.7   The movement and location of records should be controlled to ensure that a record can be easily retrieved at any time, that any outstanding issues can be dealt with, and that there is an auditable trail of record transactions.

8.8   Storage accommodation for current records should be clean and tidy, and it should prevent damage to the records. Equipment used for current records should provide storage which is safe from unauthorised access and which meets fire regulations, but which allows maximum accessibility to the information commensurate with its frequency of use. When records are no longer required for the conduct of current business, their placement in a designated records centre rather than in offices may be a more economical and efficient way to store them. Procedures for handling records should take full account of the need to preserve important information.

8.9 A contingency or business recovery plan should be in place to provide protection for records which are vital to the continued functioning of the authority.

9   Disposal Arrangements

9.1 It is particularly important under FOI that the disposal of records – which is here defined as the point in their lifecycle when they are either transferred to an archive or destroyed – is undertaken in accordance with clearly established policies which have been formally adopted by authorities and which are enforced by properly authorised staff.

Record Closure

9.2 Records should be closed as soon as they have ceased to be of active use other than for reference purposes. As a general rule, files should be closed after five years and, if action continues, a further file should be opened. An indication that a file of paper records or folder of electronic records has been closed should be shown on the record itself as well as noted in the index or database of the files/folders. Wherever possible, information on the intended disposal of electronic records should be included in the metadata when the record is created.

9.3 The storage of closed records awaiting disposal should follow accepted standards relating to environment, security and physical organization.

Appraisal Planning and Documentation

9.4 In order to make their disposal policies work effectively and for those to which the FOIA applies to provide the information required under FOI legislation, authorities need to have in place systems for managing appraisal and for recording the disposal decisions made. An assessment of the volume and nature of records due for disposal, the time taken to appraise records, and the risks associated with destruction or delay in appraisal will provide information to support an authority's resource planning and workflow arrangements.

9.5 An appraisal documentation system will ensure consistency in records appraisal and disposal. It should show what records are designated for destruction, the authority under which they are to be destroyed and when they are to be destroyed. It should also provide background information on the records, such as legislative provisions, functional context and physical arrangement. This information will provide valuable data for placing records selected for preservation into context and will enable future records managers to provide evidence of the operation of their selection policies.

Record Selection

9.6   Each authority should maintain a selection policy which states in broad terms
       the functions from which records are likely to be selected for permanent
       preservation and the periods for which other records should be retained.
       The policy should be supported by or linked to disposal schedules which
       should cover all records created, including electronic records. Schedules
       should be arranged on the basis of series or collection and should indicate
       the appropriate disposal action for all records (e.g. review after x years;
       destroy after y years).

9.7   Records selected for permanent preservation and no longer in regular use
       by the authority should be transferred as soon as possible to an archival insti-
       tution that has adequate storage and public access facilities (see Part Two
       of this Code for arrangements for bodies subject to the Public Records Acts).

9.8   Records not selected for permanent preservation and which have reached
       the end of their administrative life should be destroyed in as secure a man-
       ner as is necessary for the level of confidentiality or security markings they
       bear. A record of the destruction of records, showing their reference,
       description and date of destruction should be maintained and preserved by
       the records manager. Disposal schedules would constitute the basis of such
       a record.

9.9   If a record due for destruction is known to be the subject of a request for
       information, destruction should be delayed until disclosure has taken place
       or, if the authority has decided not to disclose the information, until the com-
       plaint and appeal provisions of the FOIA have been exhausted.

10   Management of Electronic Records

10.1   The principal issues for the management of electronic records are the same
       as those for the management of any record. They include, for example, the
       creation of authentic records, the tracking of records and disposal arrange-
       ments. However, the means by which these issues are addressed in the
       electronic environment will be different.

10.2   Effective electronic record keeping requires:

- a clear understanding of the nature of electronic records;
- the creation of records and metadata necessary to document business
  processes: this should be part of the systems which hold the records;
- the maintenance of a structure of folders to reflect logical groupings of
  records;
- the secure maintenance of the integrity of electronic records;
- the accessibility and use of electronic records for as long as required (which
  may include their migration across systems);

- the application of appropriate disposal procedures, including proce-dures for archiving; and
- the ability to cross reference electronic records to their paper counter-parts in a mixed environment.

10.3   Generic requirements for electronic record management systems are set out in the 1999 Public Record Office statement *Functional Requirements and Testing of Electronic Records Management Systems* (see http://www.pro.gov.uk/recordsmanagement/eros/invest/default.htm). Authorities are encouraged to use these, and any subsequent versions, as a model when developing their specifications for such systems.

10.4   Audit trails should be provided for all electronic information and documents. They should be kept securely and should be available for inspection by autho-rised personnel. The BSI document *Principles of Good Practice for Information Management (PD0010)* recommends audits at predetermined intervals for particular aspects of electronic records management.

10.5   Authorities should seek to conform to the provisions of BSI DISC PD0008 – *A Code of Practice for Legal Admissibility and Evidential Weight of Infor-mation Stored Electronically (2nd edn)* – especially for those records likely to be required as evidence.

PART TWO: REVIEW AND TRANSFER OF PUBLIC RECORDS

11.1   This part of the Code relates to the arrangements which authorities should follow to ensure the timely and effective review and transfer of public records. Accordingly, it is relevant only to authorities which are subject to the Public Records Acts 1958 and 1967 or to the Public Records Act (NI) 1923. The general purpose of this part of the Code is to facilitate the per-formance by the Public Record Office, the Public Record Office of Northern Ireland and other public authorities of their functions under the Freedom of Information Act.

11.2   Under the Public Records Acts, records selected for preservation may be transferred either to the Public Record Office or to places of deposit appointed by the Lord Chancellor. This Code applies to all such transfers. For guidance on which records may be transferred to which institution, and on the disposition of UK public records relating to Northern Ireland, see the Public Record Office *Acquisition Policy* (1998) and the Public Record Office *Disposition Policy* (2000).

11.3   In reviewing records for public release, authorities should ensure that pub-lic records become available to the public at the earliest possible time in accordance with the FOIA.

11.4   Authorities which have created or are otherwise responsible for public records should ensure that they operate effective arrangements to determine

a. which records should be selected for permanent preservation; and
b. which records should be released to the public.

These arrangements should be established and operated under the supervision of the Public Record Office or, in Northern Ireland, in conjunction with the Public Record Office of Northern Ireland. The objectives and arrangements for the review of records for release are described in greater detail below.

11.5   In carrying out their review of records for release to the public, authorities should observe the following points:

11.5.1   transfer to the Public Record Office must take place by the time the records are 30 years old, unless the Lord Chancellor gives authorisation for them to be retained for a longer period of time (see section 3 (4) of the Public Records Act 1958). By agreement with the Public Record Office, transfer and release may take place before 30 years;

11.5.2   review – for selection and release – should therefore take place before the records in question are 30 years old.

11.5.3   in Northern Ireland transfer under the Public Records Act (NI) 1923 to the Public Record Office of Northern Ireland is normally at 20 years.

11.6   In the case of records to be transferred to the Public Record Office or to a place of deposit appointed under section 4 of the Public Records Act 1958, or to the Public Record Office of Northern Ireland, the purpose of the review of records for release to the public is to:

• consider which information must be available to the public on transfer because no exemptions under the FOIA apply;
• consider which information must be available to the public at 30 years because relevant exemptions in the FOIA have ceased to apply;
• consider whether the information must be released in the public interest, notwithstanding the application of an exemption under the FOIA; and
• consider which information merits continued protection in accordance with the provisions of the FOIA.

11.7   If the review results in the identification of specified information which the authorities consider ought not to be released under the terms of the FOIA, the authorities should prepare a schedule identifying this information precisely, citing the relevant exemption(s), explaining why the information may not be released and identifying a date at which either release would be appropriate or a date at which the case for release should be reconsidered. Where the information is environmental information to which the exemption at section 39 of the FOIA applies, the schedule should cite the appropriate exception in the Environmental Information Regulations. This schedule must be submitted to the Public Record Office or, in Northern Ireland, to the Public Record Office of Northern Ireland prior to transfer which must be before the records containing the information are 30 years old (in the case of the Public Record Office) or 20 years old (in the case of the Public Record Office of Northern Ireland). Authorities should consider whether parts of records might be released if the sensitive information were blanked out.

11.8   In the first instance, the schedule described in 11.7 is to be submitted to the Public Record Office for review and advice. The case in favour of withholding the records for a period longer than 30 years is then considered by the Advisory Council. The Advisory Council may respond as follows:

   a. by accepting that the information may be withheld for longer than 30 years and earmarking the records for release or re-review at the date identified by the authority;
   b. by accepting that the information may be withheld for longer than 30 years but asking the authority to reconsider the later date designated for release or re-review;
   c. by questioning the basis on which it is deemed that the information may be withheld for longer than 30 years and asking the authority to reconsider the case;
   d. by advising the Lord Chancellor if it is not satisfied with the responses it receives from authorities on particular cases;
   e. by taking such other action as it deems appropriate within its role as defined in the Public Records Act.

   In Northern Ireland there are separate administrative arrangements requiring that schedules are submitted to a Sensitivity Review Group consisting of representatives of different departments. The Sensitivity Review Group has the role of advising public authorities as to the appropriateness or otherwise of releasing records.

11.9   For the avoidance of doubt, none of the actions described in this Code affects the statutory rights of access established under the FOIA. Requests for information in public records transferred to the Public Record Office or to a place of deposit appointed under section 4 of the Public Records Act 1958 or to the Public Record Office of Northern Ireland will be dealt with on a case by case basis in accordance with the provisions of the FOIA.

11.10 Where records are transferred to the Public Record Office or a place of deposit before they are 30 years old, they should be designated by the transferring department or agency for immediate release unless an exemption applies: there will be no formal review of these designations.

11.11 When an exemption has ceased to apply under section 63 of the FOIA the records will become automatically available to members of the public on the day specified in the finalised schedule (i.e. the schedule after it has been reviewed by the Advisory Council). In other cases, if the authority concerned wishes further to extend the period during which the information is to be withheld in accordance with the FOIA, it should submit a further schedule explaining the sensitivity of the information. This is to be done before the expiry of the period stated in the earlier schedule. The Public Record Office and Advisory Council will then review the schedule in accordance with the process described in paragraph 11.8 above. In Northern Ireland, Ministerial approval is required for any further extension of the stated period.

11.12 In reviewing records an authority may identify those which are appropriate for retention within the department, after they are 30 years old, under section 3(4) of the Public Records Act 1958. Applications must be submitted to the Public Record Office for review and advice. The case in favour of retention beyond the 30 year period will then be considered by the Advisory Council. The Advisory Council will consider the case for retaining individual records unless there is already in place a standing authorisation by the Lord Chancellor for the retention of a whole category of records. It will consider such applications on the basis of the guidance in chapter 9 of the White Paper *Open Government* (Cm 2290, 1993) or subsequent revisions of government policy on retention.

ANNEX A
Standards Accepted in Records Management
British Standards (BSI)

BS 4783	Storage, transportation and maintenance of media for use in data processing and information storage
BS 7799	Code of practice for information security management
BS ISO 15489-1	Information and Documentation – Records Management – Part 1: General
BSI DISC PD 0008	Code of practice for legal admissibility and evidential weight of information stored on electronic document management systems
BSI DISC PD0010	Principles of good practice for information management

BSI DISC PD0012   Guide to the practical implications of the Data Protection
                       Act 1998

Public Record Office standards for the management of public records

The Public Record Office publishes standards, guidance and toolkits on the management of public records, in whatever format, covering their entire life cycle. They are available on the Public Record Office website (http://www.pro.gov.uk/recordsmanagement).[2]

Notes

1   Note that the code refers to the 'Public Record Office', which after April 2003 became the National Archives.
2   See the updated website www.nationalarchives.gov.uk.

Appendix 2
Definitions

The Act includes several definitions. These are summarized here:

Term	Definition
Administration in the United Kingdom	• Government of the UK • Scottish Administration • Executive Committee of the Northern Ireland Assembly • National Assembly for Wales
Appropriate limit	In relation to fees this relates to the maximum cost above which the public authority does not have to comply with a request. It is the same figure, as prescribed by government, as the disproportionate cost of answering parliamentary questions (at the time of writing this was £550)
British Islands	The United Kingdom, the Channel Islands and the Isle of Man
Company	Any body corporate
Criminal proceedings	Includes: • proceedings before a court-martial constituted under the Army Act 1955, the Air Force Act 1955 or the Naval Discipline Act 1957 or a disciplinary court constituted under section 52G of the Act of 1957 • proceedings on dealing summarily with a charge under the Army Act 1955 or the Air Force Act 1955 or in summary trial under the Naval Discipline Act 1957 • proceedings before a court established by section 83ZA of the Army Act 1955, section 83ZA of the Air Force Act 1955 or section 52FF of the Naval Discipline Act 1957 (summary appeal courts) • proceedings before the Courts Martial Appeal Court • proceedings before a standing civilian court
Designated order under section 5	The Secretary of State may issue an order designating as a public authority any person not listed in Schedule 1 (except Scottish bodies)
Disbursements	Any costs reasonably incurred by a public authority in: • informing the applicant whether it holds information of the description specified in the request, and

Continued on next page

Continued

Term	Definition
	• communicating such information to the applicant
Government policy	Includes the policy of the Executive Committee of the Northern Ireland Assembly and the policy of the National Assembly for Wales
Held (by a public authority)	Includes information held by another person on behalf of the authority
Information	Must be recorded information; this includes: • on paper • electronic • photographs • sound recordings • films and videos
International court	Any international court which is not an international organization and which is established by a resolution of an international organization of which UK is a member or by an international agreement to which UK is party
International organization	Any international organization whose members include any two or more states, or any organ of such an organization
Law officers	• the Attorney-General • the Solicitor-General • the Advocate-General for Scotland • the Lord Advocate • the Solicitor-General for Scotland • the Attorney-General for Northern Ireland
Minister of the Crown	Includes a Northern Ireland Minister
Ministerial communications	Communications between: • Ministers of the Crown • Northern Ireland Ministers, including Northern Ireland junior ministers • Assembly Secretaries, including the Assembly First Secretary Proceedings of: • the Cabinet or of any committee of the Cabinet • the Executive Committee of the Northern Ireland Assembly • the Executive Committee of the National Assembly for Wales
Ministerial private office	Any part of a government department which provides personal administrative support to: • a Minister of the Crown • a Northern Ireland Minister • a Northern Ireland junior minister or any part of the administration of the National Assembly for Wales providing personal administrative support to the Assembly First Secretary or an Assembly Secretary
Northern Ireland junior minister	A member of the Northern Ireland Assembly appointed as a junior minister under section 19 of the Northern Ireland Act 1998
Offence	Includes any offence under the Army Act 1955, the Air Force Act 1955 or the Naval Discipline Act 1957

Continued on next page

Continued

Term	Definition
Prescribed costs	Any costs reasonably incurred by a public authority in: • determining whether it holds information of the description specified in the request • locating and retrieving such information, and • giving effect to any preference expressed by the applicant as to the means of communication of the information
Public authority	Any body, any other person or the holder of any office who is: • listed in Schedule 1 of the Act (see below) • designated by an order under section 5 of the Act (see above) • a publicly owned company as defined by section 6 of the Act (see below)
Publicly owned company	A company that is wholly owned by the Crown or by any pubic authority listed in Schedule 1
Request (for information)	Must: • be in writing • state the name of the applicant and an address for correspondence • describe the information requested
Schedule 1 Public authorities	This comprises seven parts: • general — government departments — Northern Ireland Assembly — National Assembly for Wales — House of Commons — House of Lords — armed forces of the Crown (except the special forces and those required to assist GCHQ) • local government — a local authority within the meaning of the Local Authority Act 1972 — others defined • the National Health Service • maintained schools and other educational institutions • police • other public bodies and offices: general (366 individually named plus any — board of visitors — housing action trust — local probation board — regional development agency — regional flood defence committee) • other public bodies and offices: Northern Ireland (84 individually named plus any — education and library board)
State	Includes the government of any state and any organ of its government; any territory outside the UK
Working day	Any day other than a Saturday, Sunday, Christmas Day, Good Friday or a day which is a bank holiday

Appendix 3
Further help and guidance

This select list points to detailed guidance on the implementation of the Freedom of Information Act and to related issues:

Websites

Office of the Information Commissioner
- www.informationcommissioner.gov.uk

Department of Constitutional Affairs (formerly the Lord Chancellor's Department)
- www.dca.gov.uk

The National Archives
- www.nationalarchives.gov.uk
- www.pro.gov.uk/recordsmanagement/standardsandguidance
- www.pro.gov.uk/recordsmanagement/electronicrecords

Advisory Group on Openness, report (1999)
- www.dca.gov.uk/foi/foiadvgp.htm

Freedom of Information Act 2000
- www.legislation.hmso.gov.uk/acts/acts2000/20000036.htm
- www.legislation.hmso.gov.uk/acts/en/2000en36.htm

Codes of Practice
- www.dca.gov.uk/foi/codepafunc.htm
- www.pro.gov.uk/accesstoinformation

Central Government guidance
• www.dca.gov.uk/foi/cgpb_guide.htm

Environmental Information Regulations
• www.sustainable-development.gov.uk/what_is_sd/transparency

National Health Service
• www.foi.nhs.uk/home.htm

Campaign for Freedom of Information
• www.cfoi.org.uk

Other guidance

• *Access to Information in Local Government* (ODPM, September 2002)
• *Publication Schemes: Guidance and Methodology* (OIC, April 2003)

For legislation, see entries in index under 'legislation'.

Index